Church Planting
and the Book of Acts

Henry Oursler and Greg Kappas
with *The Timothy Initiative Staff*

Church Planting and Book of Acts
Book Three in TTI's Foundational Curriculum

© 2012 by The Timothy Initiative

International Standard Book Number: 978-1477582619

All rights reserved. Published and Printed in the United States of America.

Library of Congress Cataloging-in-Publication Data

No part of this book covered by the copyrights heron may be reproduced or copied
in any form or by any means without written permission of the publisher.

Scripture quotations are from: The New King James Version
Copyright © 1979, 1980, 1982 by Thomas Nelson, Inc.
Used by permission. All rights reserved.

First Edition-North America
Second Edition

Acknowledgements

TTI gives special gratitude to the Docent Group and the leadership of Glenn Lucke and Jared Wilson (Docent Executive Editor for this project). The Docent writer, Pilgrim Benham is appreciated for his efforts on this large project. TTI is very grateful for Dr. Henry Oursler and his excellent rewrite of this material. Dr. Oursler is valued greatly by our TTI leadership.

TTI also gives thanks to Dr. David Nelms, our Founder/President for his vision and influence to see this New Curriculum written. Dr. Nelms has lived humbly to see you succeed greatly in Jesus Christ.

We express our gratitude for the fine, long editorial labor to TTI Executive Editor and Director, Dr. Greg Kappas and the Executive Editorial Assistant and International Director, Rev. Jared Nelms. In addition we thank the entire TTI editorial team of Dr. David Nelms, Rev. Jesse Nelms, Rev. Larry Starkey, Rev. Lou Mancari and Dr. David Nichols. Each of you has given such remarkable grace to us and now to these church planters.

TTI is greatly appreciative of the Grace Fellowship elders, pastors, administrative staff, leaders and GF family. TTI was birthed out of this "church for all nations." Thank you for your generosity in launching this exponential network of church planting movements.

TTI's Board of Directors has given us freedom and focus to excel still more. We are deeply moved by these men and women of God. Our TTI investor base of financial and prayer partners extend around the globe. These individuals, churches, ministries, networks, corporations and organizations are essential and strategic to our collective health and Kingdom impact. Thank you!

We thank the TTI Continental Directors, Regional Directors, National Directors and District/Training Center Leaders for your ministry of love and commitment. You are the ones that forge into new and current frontiers with the Gospel. You truly are our heroes.

Finally, we are forever grateful to you, the church planter. You are planting an orchard, a church planting center through your local church that will touch your region and the world with the Gospel of Jesus Christ. We are honored to serve the Lord Jesus Christ and you. You will make a difference for our great God as you multiply healthy churches for His glory. We love you and believe in you!

TTI Staff Team
October 2010

This workbook is the third of 10 workbooks which assist in equipping church planting leaders to start churches that saturate a region and help reach every man, woman and child with the Good News of our Lord. Below, is the list of this initial Curriculum.

TTI Curriculum

Workbook Number/Course:

1. Hermeneutics
2. Homiletics
3. **Church Planting (New Testament – Acts, Evangelism, Discipleship, Spiritual Life, T4T)**
4. Old Testament 1
5. Old Testament 2
6. New Testament Gospels
7. New Testament Pastoral Epistles
8. New Testament General Letters
9. Major Bible Doctrines
10. Apologetics-Church History-Spiritual Warfare

Table of Contents

Part 1 – Church Planting

Section One: Understanding Church Planting

Chapter 1 – The Great Commission 8

Chapter 2 – Planting Churches to Fulfill the Great Commission 11

Chapter 3 – Five Stages of Multiplying Healthy Churches 14

Chapter 4 – Church Planting Movements that Changed the World 23

Chapter 5 – Leadership for the Mission of Church Planting 28

Chapter 6 – What Does a Healthy Church Look Like? 32

Section Two: The Biblical Foundation of Church Planting
The Book of Acts

Chapter 7 – God Wrote a Book on Church Planting 35

Chapter 8 – Beginning in Jerusalem – Acts 1-7 39

Chapter 9 – Expanding to Judea and Samaria – Acts 8-12 49

Chapter 10 – Reaching to the Ends of the Earth – Acts 13-28 54

Chapter 11 – The World's Greatest Church Planter 67

Part 2 – Evangelism

Chapter 12 – Biblical Theology of Evangelism 72

Chapter 13 – How You Can Help Fulfill the Great Commission 77

Chapter 14 – Prayer and Evangelism 81

Chapter 15 – The Evangelist and the Missional Church 87

Part 3 – Discipleship

Chapter 16 – What Does It Mean to Make Disciples? 89

Chapter 17 – Misconceptions about Discipleship 95

Chapter 18 – Discipleship: Jesus' Plan to Reach the World 99

Chapter 19 – The Disciple-Making Pastor & Disciple-Making Church 104

Chapter 20 – How Jesus Discipled His Men 108

Chapter 21 – Growing Disciples to Maturity 111

Chapter 22 – Applying the Basics of Discipleship 114

Appendix – Disciple Making Disciples 118

Endnotes 134

Introduction

NOTES

Do not plant a church! Those were the words one of my mentors spoke to me. Actually the full statement he made was: *Do not plant a church unless you are absolutely sure that God has called you to do it!*

At first those words did not make sense. After all, I had been in ministry for twenty four years. I had served as a missionary to college campuses around North America. I had lectured on over *100* university campuses. I had been involved in evangelism and discipleship ministries around the world. My wife and I had spoken at family and marriage conferences to over *100,000* people world-wide. I had been the teaching pastor at a church that averaged *1,500* people per week. I had even taught at church planting conferences! Why shouldn't I plant a church? And yet I was being told: *Do not plant a church!*

I've come to realize that there is much wisdom behind that statement. Church planting is one of the most exciting, challenging and fulfilling ministries there is. And yet it is also filled with land-mines, dangers and spiritual battles.

I went ahead and planted a church…because I was absolutely convinced that God called me to do it. I did so somewhat reluctantly. In fact, I gave God every opportunity to "change His mind." He didn't. And I began one of the greatest adventures of my ministry experience.[1]

And now, you are beginning that same exciting adventure. You have likely begun – or will soon begin – gathering a core group of people in your village, town or city. You will pray for them and with them. You will disciple them and train them in ministry skills. You will teach God's Word to them. You will point them in the direction they should go, both individually and as a church. And you will begin to make a difference in your community through personal and group evangelism efforts to reach people with the Gospel of Jesus Christ. God Himself has put this dream and calling in your heart. That's thrilling!

May I give a warning at this point? Satan and his demonic forces will not ignore your efforts. The Prince of Darkness will use his strategies of discouragement, persecution, division and temptation to keep you from achieving God's dream for your ministry. Resist him. Stand firm in the faith. Fulfill the calling God has given you – to help reach your part of the world through the planting of a church that will plant other churches to do the very same thing.

This training book is at the heart of your mission. In this book I talk about three essential components of ministry: (*1*) Church planting, (*2*) Evangelism and (*3*) Discipleship. Included in the section on church planting is an extended commentary on the book of *Acts* from the perspective of a church planter. I have given my life to see these things happen around the world. And it is thrilling that you are now a part of The Timothy Initiative's ministry of reproductive church planting.

I would like to pray for you right now. In my prayer, I am going to use Moses' words from *Numbers 6:24-26*. It is my prayer for you now as you read this book, tomorrow as you apply its teachings in your church planting ministry, and for many days in the future as you reproduce your efforts by planting multiplying churches that will plant other multiplying churches.

May God bless you and keep you. May He cause His face to shine upon you and be gracious to you. May the Lord Himself lift up His countenance on you and give you peace.

Assignment:

Are you sure God has called you to be a church planter? How do you know that? Write out in specific terms how God called you to be a church planter. If you are not yet sure, what are the questions and doubts you have about church planting?

Chapter 1
The Great Commission

Introduction

If you ask Christians to turn in their Bibles to *The Great Commission*, most of them will locate *Matthew 28:18-20*. However, that is only one of at least five times Jesus gave His disciples the command to go into all the world and proclaim the Gospel. Let's begin by taking a fresh look at the Great Commission in all five passages.[2]

> **Assignment:**
>
> Read the following Great Commission references and make notes about what is unique and different in each passage. *John 20:21; Mark 16:15; Matthew 28:18-20; Luke 24:44-49; Acts 1:8*

What is a Commission? A mission is a task we have been given to accomplish. A co-mission is a task we have been given to accomplish in partnership with someone else as a partner. Jesus is our partner in the *Great Commission*.

Ephesians 3:10 tells us that God's plan is that His manifold wisdom might be made known through the church. How will the world know of His manifold wisdom? By you and me obeying the Great Commission and going into the entire world preaching the Gospel.

Let's take a look at each of these commands and note how they interrelate to form a unique, whole message.

1. We Are Sent – *John 20:21*

    A. *John 20:21* emphasizes the fact that we are sent into the world.

    B. We serve the God who sends His people to all cultures in the world.

    C. With God, there are no locked doors. He opens the doors so the Gospel may be proclaimed everywhere.

    D. There are many different cultures in the world. We are sent to all of them. Therefore, we must not only know God, but also to understand the culture(s) to which He is sending us.

    E. Church planting is the key to spreading the Gospel.

    F. The Great Commission is always accompanied by the presence of the Holy Spirit or the promise of His presence with us.

2. To Everyone Everywhere – *Mark 16:15*

A. *Mark 16:15* emphasizes the fact that we are sent to reach every man, woman and child in the world.

B. However, we all have circles of influence in our lives made up of people we know, people we live nearby, our family and friends, and people we work with.

C. Churches also have circles of influence – and they are accountable to reach the people in those circles.

D. In Paul's ministry, he said *imitate me*! What did Paul do? He preached the Gospel everywhere he went.

E. In the book of *Acts*, Paul demonstrated many unique approaches to reach unique people groups. In Paul's ministry, there were different beginning points. But he always ended up at the same ending point – preaching the death and resurrection of Christ.

3. With A Strategy – *Matthew 28:18-20*

A. In *Matthew 28:18-20*, Jesus gives us a strategy by which we can accomplish the Great Commission.

B. This is the longest, most familiar, and most extensive statement about the Great Commission.

C. Jesus said He has all authority in heaven and earth

D. He commanded us to make disciples. *Make disciples* is the main verb in the Great Commission in *Matthew 28*, indicating that its action is the major focus of the command. There are three words that qualify how we are to make disciples:[3]
- *Going* – this speaks of evangelism and telling others how they can know Jesus personally.
- *Baptizing* – baptism is how people become a part of a local church. They are now relationally connected to others who can help them grow as a follower of Jesus.
- *Teaching* – this is the educational aspect of the Great Commission. We are to teach new believers all that Jesus commanded us. As a result, they will become personally equipped and will begin to mature as a disciple.

4. Telling a Message – *Luke 24:44-49*

A. *Luke 22:44-49* describes the message we are to proclaim. We are to tell others the Gospel – which involves repentance from sin and faith in Jesus.

B. There is no other message in heaven and on earth by which men can be saved – *Acts 4:12*.

C. *2 Corinthians 5:18-20* tells us that we are ambassadors representing God to the world and we are to proclaim the message of reconciliation.

5. Empowered for the Task – *Acts 1:8*

A. *Acts 1:8* answers the question, how are believers equipped for this mission? The power of the Holy Spirit is absolutely necessary. The Holy Spirit is the One who makes our witnessing effective.

B. We must be focused on the right things. *Acts 1:5-7* tells us that *the right thing* to be preoccupied with is not prophecy and knowing when Jesus will return. Rather, it is the fulfillment of the Great Commission He has given us. We must trust the work of the Holy Spirit in the lives of new believers, new pastors, and new churches as they carry on the legacy of ministry and mission Jesus established.

C. We must be focused on the right places. Jesus talks about Jerusalem, Judea, Samaria and the ends of the earth. There is a logical progression and strategy involved here.

Conclusion

The summary of this chapter is: *We are sent... to everyone everywhere... with a strategy... telling a message... empowered for the task.*

> **Assignment:**
>
> Memorize the summary statement written above.
>
> List three new insights you learned about The Great Commission. Why are these important to you?

Chapter 2
Planting Churches to Fulfill the Great Commission

Introduction

Planting new churches is the single most crucial strategy for the numerical growth of the Body of Christ in any area, and the continual corporate renewal and revival of the existing churches in that area. Nothing else – not large scale evangelistic meetings, outreach programs, nor church renewal processes – will have the consistent impact of dynamic, extensive church planting. This is a very strong statement. But to those who have done any study at all, it is not even controversial.[4]

Why is church planting so crucially important?

1. We Plant Churches Because The Bible Tells Us To

A. Jesus' challenge to the first-century disciples was to plant churches. The Great Commission in *Matthew 28:18-20* is not just a call to evangelize, but to *make disciples* and *baptize* them in the faith. In *Acts* and elsewhere, it is clear that baptism means incorporation into a worshipping community with accountability and boundaries (cf. *Acts 2:41-47*).

The major way to be truly sure you are increasing the number of Christians in a village or town is to increase the number of churches. This is why a leading missions expert can say, *planting new churches is the most effective evangelistic methodology known under heaven.*[5]

B. Paul's whole strategy was to plant churches in cities across Asia Minor. The greatest missionary in history had a rather simple, two-fold strategy. First, he went into the largest city of the region (cf. *Acts 16:9, 12*), and second, he planted churches in each village, town or city (cf. *Titus 1:5 – appoint elders in every town*). Once Paul had done that, he could say that he had *fully preached* the Gospel in a region and that he had *no more work* to do there (cf. *Romans 15:19, 23*).

Paul understood that the way to most permanently influence a country was through its chief cities, and the way to most permanently influence a city was to plant churches in it. Once he had accomplished this in a city, he moved on. He knew that the rest that needed to happen would follow.

2. We Plant Churches To Fulfill The Great Commission

    A. New churches best reach new generations, new residents to an area, and new people groups.

    B. New churches are the best way to reach the unchurched. Around the world, new churches reach the lost more effectively than established churches.[6]

    C. This means that the average new congregation will bring *6-8* times more new people into the life of the Body of Christ than an older congregation of the same size. New congregations focus on the needs of its non-members simply to get off the ground. Many of the leaders of new churches come very recently from the ranks of the un-churched. This results in the congregation being more sensitive to the concerns of the non-believer. Also, in the first two years of our Christian walk, we have far more close, face-to-face relationships with non-Christians than we do later. Thus a congregation filled with people fresh from the ranks of the un-churched will have the power to invite and attract many more non-believers into the events and life of the church than will the members of the typical established body.[7]

One church advisor talks about *The 1% Rule*. Each year any association of churches should plant new congregations at the rate of *1%* of their existing total. Otherwise, that association will be in decline. That is just *maintenance*. If an association wants to grow by *50%* or more, it must plant *2-3%* per year.[8]

What does this mean practically? The only wide scale way to bring in many new Christians to the Body of Christ in a permanent way is to plant new churches.

3. We Plant Churches to Bring Renewal to the Body of Christ

The planting of new churches in a city is one of the very best ways to revitalize many older churches in the vicinity and renew the whole Body of Christ. Why?

    A. New churches bring new ideas to the whole Body.

    B. New churches are one of the best ways to identify creative, strong leaders for the whole Body. In older congregations, leaders emphasize tradition, tenure, routine, and kinship ties. New congregations, on the other hand, attract a higher percentage of venturesome people who value creativity, risk, innovation and future orientation. Many of these men and women would never be attracted or compelled into significant ministry apart from the appearance of these new bodies. Often older churches "box out" many people with strong leadership skills who cannot work in more traditional settings. New churches thus attract and harness many people whose gifts would otherwise not be utilized in the work of the Body.[9]

    C. New churches challenge other churches to self-examination. The "success" of new churches often challenges older congregations in general to evaluate themselves in substantial ways. Sometimes it is only in contrast with a new church that older churches can finally define their own vision, specialties, and identity. Often the growth of the new congregation gives the older churches hope that real growth can happen, and may even bring about humility and repentance from negative attitudes.

4. We Plant Churches Because We Are Kingdom-Minded

A. When a new congregation is birthed by an older *mother* congregation, excitement and renewal occur in the established church. They have a sense of vision, mission and accomplishment in the planting of this new work.

B. The established church also experiences a partnership in outreach and impact.

C. Our attitude to new church development is a test of whether our mindset is geared to our own church, or to the overall health and prosperity of the Kingdom of God in the region.

Conclusion

Jesus has established the mission and strategy of planting new churches. New church planting is the primary way that we can be sure we are going to increase the number of believers in a town or city. It is also one of the best ways to renew the whole Body of Christ. It is the Biblical way to fulfill The Great Commission.

> **Assignment:**
>
> Read *Acts 2:41-47*. What do these verses tell you about evangelism and the early church? Why was evangelism so important for them? Why should it be important for you as a church planter?

Chapter 3
Five Stages for Multiplying Healthy Churches[10]

Introduction

I am committed to planting healthy churches – churches that are balanced and committed to Biblical principles. I believe that if a church is healthy, it will grow. It's the same way with our children. Linda and I never once told our children, *you must grow*! We simply made sure they were healthy: that they had good, nutritious meals, that they were free from disease and sickness, and that they got plenty of exercise and sleep. And guess what? They grew! It was *natural* for them to do so.

This chapter will discuss five specific stages involved in planting a church. As you progress through this material, ask yourself, *where am I in these stages? What must I do next?*

1. Relating and Reaching

Jesus said, *I will build My church*. Church planting is the most effective way of reaching lost people – and the most effective way of incorporating those new converts into a local body of believers. Statistics show that new churches are thirty times more effective in adding people into God's Kingdom than established, older churches.

Once a church planter has determined his call from God and is approved through an assessment process, what are the next steps in relating to his community and reaching lost people for Jesus?

   A. Developing a Spiritual Foundation

   As the church planter, you must walk with Jesus. Your life must be devoted to Him. We will talk more about this in *Part 4* of this book. Your church cannot grow spiritually unless you are a qualified spiritual leader.

Assignment:

Identify the one or two areas in your life where you really need to grow spiritually to be the man God uses to build His church. Make these areas a matter of consistent prayer over the next twelve months.

   B. Gathering an Intercession Team

   The greatest thing you can do for your new church effort is to recruit people to pray for you. Every Christian you meet becomes a potential prayer partner. Make a list of all of the people praying for you and your new church... and keep them informed about specific prayer requests they can pray back to the Father.

Assignment:

Seek to enlist Christians who will pray at least five minutes each week for your new church plant.

   C. Contacting the Community

      Every community, no matter how large or small, has influential leaders. If possible, make them aware of your new church plant. Go visit them and tell them of your plans. Describe the goals and plans you have. And invite them to join you as you begin worship services or your small group, depending on how you start your church. For those of you who are ministering in environments that are openly hostile to the Gospel, we recognize that this is not possible. However, God will still open doors for you to network with people of similar interest in your community.

Assignment:

Who are the leaders you are going to contact in your community? When will you meet with them? Once you have met with them once, continue to build and develop a relationship with them – and, if your cultural situation allows it, keep inviting them to your public worship services or small group.

   D. Casting Seeds

      Share the Gospel wherever you go. Let everyone know what you are doing – and why you are doing it. Develop the habit of sharing the Gospel with everyone you meet. If your environment is hostile to the Gospel, then use wisdom with whom you share Jesus Christ. Timing is important!

Assignment:

Who will you share the Gospel with today? Who will you share the Gospel with tomorrow?

   E. Creating Small Groups

      As your church grows in numbers, you should establish small groups within the church. Real life-change takes place in the context of small groups. You should start several small groups even before you begin public worship. Teach these new believers and seekers about the basics of the Christian faith, how they can have a daily Quiet Time, how they can pray, and how they can study the Bible for themselves.

NOTES

The *Disciple Making Disciples* (DMD) material located in Appendix I will give you great examples of how to do this.

> **Assignment:**
>
> What materials will you use to lead your small group? Who will you recruit to be in the group? Who will you train to lead future small groups?

2. Establishing and Connecting

Stage 2 moves into the basic systems and system designs of this new church plant. At the base of all we do, even in these beginning stages, we are concentrating on the reproduction and multiplication of godly influencers for Jesus Christ.

Stage 2 unfolds vision and values of the new plant, criteria for the launch team, getting a crowd for worship, designing and developing an attraction ministry, turning the crowd into a church and establishing criteria for new church membership. This is best summarized with the following:

A. Developing the Team to Help You Start the Church

You cannot start a church by yourself. As soon as possible, find a man or woman of peace and you will begin to see many in your village or towns respond to the Gospel. You must recruit and train other gifted leaders to help you. The number one mistake new church planters make is trying to do everything themselves. Not only can you *not* do everything by yourself – but if you attempt to do so, you are robbing others of the joy of serving.

In some cases, you may be the only Christian in your village. Don't despair. God has sent you there as His representative. Look for the man or woman of peace. Share the Gospel with others and trust God that these new converts will be the ones to help you start the church.

> **Assignment:**
>
> Who is on the team to help you launch the church? Some of these will be your key leaders in years to come. Build them as leaders. Train them as servants.

B. Designing Your Worship Services

For those of you who are planting churches in towns and cities where they may grow larger, you must give good thought to how you will structure your worship services. Use music that is culturally relevant to those you are trying to reach. Who will lead that music? Where will you meet? Who will help serve with you?

If you are planting a church in a rural village, your worship will be more relaxed and informal. The most important elements will be a sense of genuine community and a discipleship process that builds leaders. Your love for others will draw many to the Savior (*Joh. 13:34, 35*).

> **Assignment:**
>
> What other elements of worship are important to you? Think through the specifics of all that is involved.

C. Determining Membership

Membership in a local church is a very key issue. It must be taken seriously. And that begins with you having sure convictions about what membership involves.

Basic requirements for church membership usually include a credible personal testimony of how that person came to saving faith in Jesus; water baptism; and a commitment to the vision and fellowship of the local church.

> **Assignment:**
>
> Determine the answers to the following questions: What are your requirements for membership? How will people join your church? What will be the responsibilities of church membership?

Stage 2 involves organization and planning. The leader who manages to move through *Stage 1* will become stuck in *Stage 2* without someone who is administratively gifted to assist in these key areas. *Stage 2* not only calls for a church planting team to arise, but the right kind of balanced team with essential gift mix.

The Biblical exhortations in *Ephesians 4:7-16* become important in this stage. The new church will eventually have equippers who are apostles, prophets, evangelists, pastors and teachers. You will need to begin to build disciples, training and equipping them in accordance with the gifts God has given them. This will be the main focus of *Stage 3*.

Stage 2 is a hinge stage that can impact momentum in a positive or negative way, as people become trained and equipped in *Stage 3*. To solidify this hinge of *Stage 2*, there needs to be security and patience from the church planting leaders to not rush through *Stage 1* and attempt to move into *Stage 2* prematurely. *Stage 2* can take a long time – or it can pass rather quickly. This is the stage where many church planters make big and potentially fatal decisions. The cultural and social rush to begin Sunday morning worship celebrations (or another time of the week in a different context) can move things further along in perception than where the new plant is at in reality.

3. Training and Equipping

Everyone needs training and equipping...especially church planters and ministry teams. In this section we concentrate on equipping believers in our church to move toward spiritual maturity and ministry effectiveness. Keep in mind that our goal is not simply to mature them, but to equip them to serve. Built on the principles from *Ephesians 4:11-16*, we must equip the saints for works of service. Paul told his protégée, Timothy, *And the things you have heard from me among many witnesses, commit these to faithful men who will be able to teach others also* (2 Timothy 2:2).

    A. Developing Mature Believers

    God has called the leadership of the church to move people toward maturity (*Ephesians 4*). You will read more about discipleship in *Part 3* of this book. All believers need to learn to be self-feeders in the Word of God. They must develop in the basic spiritual disciplines discussed later in this workbook.

Assignment:

Begin by identifying where the people in your congregation are spiritually. What are their needs? How can you help them grow?

    B. Discovering Spiritual Gifts

    God has given spiritual gifts to each believer. They are to be used for the building up of the Body of Christ. Study the basic passages of spiritual gifts, including *Romans 12:1-7, 1 Corinthians 12-14, 1 Peter 4:7-11* and *Ephesians 4:7-16*. Determine how the new believers and existing Christians can be trained, and discover God's eternal endowments in their lives.

Assignment:

Do you know what your spiritual gifts are? How can you encourage others to learn more about their gifts and develop them for God's glory? Discuss.

    C. Developing Disciple-makers

    It is not only important to build disciples, but it is critical that we build disciple-makers. Reproducing disciples is the mandate, method and mission of Jesus.

Assignment:

Read *2 Timothy 2:2*. How are you training your leaders to pass on spiritual truth to those they are discipling? Discuss.

D. Defining Spiritual Stewardship

Jesus talked much about money, stewardship and having a spirit of generosity. You must model this yourself and teach on it boldly. Individuals and churches are noted by their generosity. Be a person who gives *23%* or more of your income to the Lord. (This was the pattern of the Old Testament and our call to grace-giving should compel us to give even more). Challenge your congregation as a whole to give *50%* of the church's budget to the Lord and His work outside of your local body.

Assignment:

Read *2 Corinthians 8:1- 7*. What does this teach about money? How will you faithfully instruct your congregation on financial stewardship? Discuss.

If you don't help define spiritual maturity, place people in ministry, make disciples, and teach on giving and stewardship, then you really don't have a church. Even if there are large numbers attending, it really is not a church in the eyes of the Lord. Whether large or small, you must have a strong leadership base. This is the emphasis of *Stage 3*.

I find it so interesting that this is where Jesus spent the bulk of His time. He loved, encouraged, inspired, trained and equipped His men. He started His ministry there and He ended His ministry there. It is true that there were attraction points with large crowds, but even then, there were often hard words from our Master. Many church planting efforts invest large amounts of energy and funds towards attracting and motivating the crowd. We spend so much effort on Sunday mornings that little time and focus is left for training and equipping leaders.

We must look in the mirror and see what Jesus sees. Are we so consumed in making the new church survive by simply drawing the crowd? Or will we understand the need for a God-honoring ministry, while also training and equipping leaders like Barnabas and Saul did in *Acts 11* and *13*? The church at Antioch of Syria understood the need for both a celebration of worship and individual training and equipping. This is crucial to church health.

Stage 3 naturally leads to *Stage 4*. As leaders emerge, they need to be led and coached dynamically. There is a need to be intentional in leadership development, to handle crisis and conflict properly, and to develop partnerships regionally, nationally and internationally. Emerging leaders are needed for multiplying new churches. You must consider what it means to be a church planting center. In all of this, determining more effective criteria for measuring church health becomes apparent.

What if God calls you to move on and start additional churches or to another ministry? Who will be the next group of leaders to take over? Who will you leave in leadership if this happens as it did with Barnabas and Saul in *Acts 13:1-3*? They had a team to continue this great work of God. Will you? That is the burning question of *Stage 4*. Will you and your team be intentional to reproduce and multiply? *Stage 4* is time for this to come to completion?

4. Leading and Coaching

Learning from Jesus, the apostle Paul spent much of his ministry leading and coaching church planters, starting new churches, and teaching the Word of God. Paul also gave new revelation through Scripture and emphasizing the need for good Biblical and theological thinking. As church planters we need to follow his passion and model. He understood and taught the Revelational (faith), Missional (hope) and Relational (love) balance.

As we begin *Stage 4*, remember the necessity to be teachable. Great leaders are developed when they are teachable. In this stage we examine six aspects of leading and coaching:

   A. Weathering the Crisis Points

   Stage 4 begins with handling conflict appropriately. Early in his ministry Paul had to deal with this very thing. In *Acts 15* we see large amounts of doctrinal, spiritual and emotional conflict. Paul and Barnabas deal with whether the Gospel is simply for the Jews or if it is also for the Gentiles.

   How we handle conflict in our personal lives will spill over into how we do the same in the ministry. Do you take time to process things that happen to you personally and in your new church plant? Do you pray through things and seek God's wisdom on how to respond?

Assignment:

How have you seen leaders deal with conflict? Was it positive and constructive – or did it result in disunity and destruction? How will you handle conflict? Discuss.

   B. Becoming a Church Planting Church

   It is essential that you begin thinking and praying about starting other churches early in the life of your church. The longer you wait to plant your first church, the less likely it is that you will ever reproduce yourself.

   Studies show that a church that does not plant a new church within three years is less likely to plant churches. Like an orchard of trees, your new church plant will become a church planting center, with a vision to multiply churches consistently.

Assignment:

What is your vision for starting other churches? When will you do this? Where will those churches be located? Who will lead them? Though you may not have all the answers at this point, you must begin praying and planning toward these goals. Discuss.

Reproducing and multiplying healthy churches is at God's heart. *Stage 5* is not simply a stage. It is the base for the other four stages. *Stage 5* reminds us why we start churches in the first place. The Holy Spirit is the One who gave the calling to start multiple churches (*Acts 13:1-3*.) This stage must exist in your heart long before *Stage 1* begins.

Those who have this commitment to multiplication from the beginning become part of a church planting movement. Remember: starting multiple churches is not the ultimate goal. We are called to saturate a region with the Good News of Jesus Christ, by being revelational, missional and relational. We are called to saturate the nations of the world with the Gospel. This calling brings pleasure to the Father and allows us to better glorify Him.

Stage 5 also reminds us that we flow back to *Stage 1* in starting a new church that starts multiple churches. The process and cycle continues as we serve our Lord with a holy passion, a godly calling and insightful assessment.

5. Reproducing and Multiplying

As a church and ministry face the tough areas of Leading and Coaching in *Stage 4*, inevitably the initial values of reproduction and multiplication return to the forefront. Critical thoughts come to the surface again and again. These questions can be voiced publicly or quietly understood. These matters are felt deeply by multiple church staff and leaders such as deacons and elders, as well as the congregation at large. They center on:

  A. Saturating a Region with the Gospel

  Whether you are in a village in the countryside or a large city, your vision must be to saturate that region with the Gospel, insuring that every man, woman and child has repeated opportunities to hear about Jesus. If you live in a large region, divide it into circles of accountability. If it is a small region, be sure to think through how you can saturate the area with the Gospel.

  One way you can start is by *prayer walking* your area for the Gospel. You can do this by yourself or with others. Simply begin walking around the area, praying for the people and families you see. Pray that they will come to know Christ. Pray that your church – and other churches – will greatly influence this area for Jesus. And pray that the glory of the Gospel will be known throughout the entire region.

Assignment:

Do you really care that every man, woman and child in your area of responsibility hears the Gospel? How does that burden you? What are you going to do about it?

B. Insuring Rapid Reproduction

As soon as God provides qualified leaders, we must start new churches. Don't wait until all the conditions are right – because all the conditions may never be right. A loss of rapid reproduction is a gain for Satan and his evil forces. As regions grow in populations and churches do not, you have actually added to the lostness of your region. We want to reduce lostness by the grace of Jesus Christ.

> **Assignment:**
>
> Who are you training that can plant and lead these new churches? How are you training them?

C. Proper Care for Leadership

Insuring rapid reproduction of new churches means that we will need a continually growing supply of leaders. You must learn to care and shepherd these leaders of leaders. It has been said that people do not care how much you know until they know how much you care for them.

> **Assignment:**
>
> The best way to care for leaders is to ask yourself: *What did I need when I was just starting out as a leader?* It is likely they need the same things. Discuss.

D. Church Planting Centers and Networks

Your church should seek to ultimately become a church planting center that trains and resources new churches and networks of new churches throughout your region. This will move you into a new and greater dimension of leadership than ever before.

This expansion of the Kingdom of God takes ground back from the enemy that he has gained over the years. Your mission and vision must include seeing your church as the beginning of an orchard for Jesus Christ.

> **Assignment:**
>
> Your ability to lead leaders and to continually express vision and direction is very important. How are you doing in those areas right now? How do you need to grow so that you can move into this greater dimension of leadership?

Chapter 4
Church Planting Movements that Changed the World

1. Five Characteristics of Missionary and Gospel-Centered Movements

In his helpful book *Movements That Change the World*, author Steve Addison identifies five characteristics of missionary and Gospel-centered movements:[11]

- A. White-hot faith: *Missionary movements begin with men and women who encounter the living God and surrender in loving obedience to His call.*[12]

- B. Commitment to a cause: A commitment to the cause of Christ and His Gospel leads people to become *fearless and uncompromising agents of transformation in this world.*[13]

- C. Contagious relationships: A missionary movement will be *at home in the existing culture and yet radically distinct from it. Movements spread quickly through preexisting networks of relationships.* In other words, an isolationist form of Christianity will never advance a movement of God.[14]

- D. Rapid mobilization: Missionary movements that spread rapidly are not *centrally planned, funded, or controlled*. I would add this is why young people have been so instrumental in the spread of Gospel movements. They do not need tremendous structure; they need a cause and a direction and then to be released.[15]

- E. Adaptive methods: From the earliest missionary journeys that went to Europe until today, methods change even though the Gospel never changes. *The forms changed to fit the context and to serve the needs of an expanding movement while the unchanging Gospel remained at the center of the movement.*[16]

While many today think of Christianity in its organized and institutional sense (denominations, missions agencies, etc.), in its essence Christianity is still today what it was in its inception: a movement. It is a movement focusing on God's movement in the world, in particular through the person and work of Jesus Christ, God's Son. It is a movement reflective of God's greater movement to create all we see and know, and its movement toward God's greater purposes. It is a movement for which countless followers of Christ have suffered and died.

It is a movement centered not on a Western lifestyle or on what we can get from God. No, it is a movement focused on the salvation offered in Jesus Christ through His work on the cross, dying as a substitute for our own sin, and through His glorious resurrection.

NOTES

This movement calls its followers to spread its message to all people, to every tribe and tongue. And the more the leaders and followers of the movement do just that, the more it resembles the very ideal given in the pages of Scripture.

Unfortunately, in the Western church the tendency has been to focus more about buildings and services and programs than lifestyle and mission and passion. In the history of the church you can see it moves back and forth between institutionalism and stagnation, and then finds a fresh passion for the Gospel and a renewed focus on advancing the church and the good news we have to share.

Think about the amazing Gospel, both in terms of its great story (creation-fall-redemption-new creation), and with a focus on the work of Jesus through the cross and His resurrection. There is in the middle of our faith a bloody cross. And from that cross we have been given a cause. Is Jesus the center of everything in your life as He is the center of creation, Scripture, history, and redemption? Is He the center of your economic world? Your relational world? Your private world?

2. An Analogy

A well-known story illustrates what happens when a good movement with a mission loses her focus and becomes simply an organization without focus and direction. The story is called The Parable of the Lifesaving Station:

> *On a dangerous seacoast where shipwrecks often occur there was a once a crude little life-saving station. The building was just a hut, and there was only one boat, but the few devoted members kept a constant watch over the sea, and with no thought for themselves, they went out day or night tirelessly searching for the lost.*
>
> *Many lives were saved by this wonderful little station, so that it became famous. Some of those who were saved, and various others in the surrounding areas, wanted to become associated with the station and give of their time and money and effort for the support of its work. New boats were bought and new crews were trained. The little life-saving station grew.*
>
> *Some of the new members of the life-saving station were unhappy that the building was so crude and so poorly equipped. They felt that a more comfortable place should be provided as the first refuge of those saved from the sea. So they replaced the emergency cots with beds and put better furniture in an enlarged building. Now the life-saving station became a popular gathering place for its members, and they redecorated it beautifully and furnished it as a sort of club. Less of the members were now interested in going to sea on lifesaving missions, so they hired life boat crews to do this work.*
>
> *The mission of life-saving was still talked about, but most were too busy or lacked the necessary commitment to take part in the life-saving activities personally. About this time a large ship was wrecked off the coast, and the hired crews brought in boat loads of cold, wet, and half-drowned people.*
>
> *They were dirty and sick, and some of them had black skin, and some spoke a strange language, and the beautiful new club was considerably messed up. So the property committee immediately had a shower house built outside the club where victims of shipwreck could be cleaned up before coming inside.*

At the next meeting, there was a split in the club membership. Most of the members wanted to stop the club's life-saving activities as being unpleasant and a hindrance to the normal life pattern of the club.

But some members insisted that life-saving was their primary purpose and pointed out that they were still called a life-saving station. But they were finally voted down and told that if they wanted to save the life of all the various kinds of people who were shipwrecked in those waters, they could begin their own life-saving station down the coast. They did.

As the years went by, the new station experienced the same changes that had occurred in the old. They evolved into a club and yet another life-saving station was founded. If you visit the seacoast today you will find a number of exclusive clubs along that shore. Shipwrecks are still frequent in those waters, only now most of the people drown.[17]

3. Church Planting Movements Around the World

In Europe:

In 1999, among the refugees in the Netherlands, Church Planting Movement practitioners reported 45 new church starts in a single year.

In 1958, the Gypsies of Spain and France baptized 3,000 new believers, and then more than tripled their number over the next six years. By 1979 there were 30-40,000 Gypsy church members with 150,000 attending worship.[18]

In Latin America:

An Assembly of God church in Guayaquil, Ecuador has 7,000 church members in 2,000 cell groups.

The Living Water Church in Lima, Peru weekly hosts 600 cell groups and 7,000 members. René Peñalba's Love Alive Church in Tegucigalpa, Honduras, is home to 7,000 worshipers meeting in 1,000 cell groups.

Begun in 1983, César Castellanos's cell church in Bogotá, Colombia has grown to more than 20,000 cells and 100,000 members.

In San Salvador, Sergio Solórzano's Elim church claims 116,000 people regularly attending 5,300 cell groups. Each Sunday morning, the church rents 600 city buses to transport cell members to the weekly celebration services.

In 1990 Cuban Baptists reported 235 churches. By 2000 the number had grown to 4,000 churches.

Evangelicals across Cuba are on track to see 100,000 churches with 1 million baptized believers. Church leaders estimate that 70% of the country's 13 million residents have received a Jesus Film, New Testament, and/or personal witness to Jesus Christ.[19]

NOTES

In Africa:

Across the continent of Africa, Christianity has exploded from less than 9 million in 1900 to over 470 million in 2010.[20]

In the Muslim World:

In an Al-Jazeera interview Libyan Sheikh Ahmed al-Katani stated, "In every hour, 667 Muslims convert to Christianity. Every day, 16,000 Muslims convert to Christianity. Every year, 6 million Muslims convert to Christianity."[21]

A movement in North Africa grows from 22,000 baptized believers in 2003 to more than 160,000 in 2009. More Iranians have come to Christ since 1979 than in the thousand years that preceded it.

A movement in South Asia was assessed in 2002 with more than 125,000 baptized Muslim-background believers.[22]

Across China:

In China, more than 30,000 new believers are baptized every day.

A Church Planting Movement in a northern Chinese province sees 20,000 new believers and 500 new churches planted in less than five years.

In Henan Province Christianity explodes from less than a million to more than five million believers in only eight years.

Chinese Christians in Qing'an County of Heilongjiang Province plant 236 new churches in a single month.

In southern China a Church Planting Movement produces more than 90,000 baptized believers in 920 house churches in eight years' time.[23]

In India:

In Tamil Nadu, Assemblies of God leaders adopt a vision to plant 12,000 new churches over the next ten years.

A Church Planting Movement among Bhojpuri-speaking people results in more than 11,000 new churches and some 1,000,000 new believers.[24]

In the T4T Movement:

A recent movement started in China in 2001, has produced the fastest growing Church Planting Movement in the world to date. They have already seen nearly two million baptisms and more than 80,000 new church starts in less than a decade.[25]

Assignment:

Have you thought of Christianity in terms of her institutions (buildings, organizations, etc.) rather than as a movement?

How would your life change if you saw yourself as someone given totally to the movement of God in the world?

NOTES

Chapter 5
Leadership for the Mission of Church Planting

Introduction

There are three critical elements in accomplishing any task: knowing your *mission*, having the right *strategy*, and being directed by qualified *leaders*.

If the Great Commission is truly our calling (see *chapter 1*), our *mission* is defined. And if planting churches is the most effective way to fulfill the Great Commission (see *chapter 2*), our *strategy* is also defined. Now, however, comes the third critical element: qualified *leadership*.

God has ordained elders to lead the church and deacons to serve the church. Other workbooks in the TTI training series deal with these two offices. However, there is an additional passage of Scripture we must consider. Read the words of *Ephesians 4:7-16*.

> *But to each one of us grace was given according to the measure of Christ's gift. Therefore He says: "When He ascended on high, He led captivity captive, and gave gifts to men." (Now this "He ascended" – what does it mean but that He also first descended into the lower parts of the earth? He who descended is also the One who ascended far above all the heavens, that He might fill all things)."*
>
> *And He gave some to be apostles, some prophets, some evangelists, and some pastors and teachers, for the equipping of the saints for the work of ministry, for the edifying of the body of Christ, till we all come to the unity of the faith and of the knowledge of the Son of God, to a perfect man, to the measure of the stature of the fullness of Christ; that we should no longer be children, tossed to and fro and carried about with every wind of doctrine, by the trickery of men, in the cunning craftiness of deceitful plotting, but speaking the truth in love, may grow up in all things into Him who is the head – Christ – from whom the whole body, joined and knit together by what every joint supplies, according to the effective working by which every part does its share, causes growth of the body for the edifying of itself in love.*

In *verse 11*, Paul describes five roles within the leadership of the church: apostles, prophets, evangelists, pastors (whom we will refer to as Shepherds) and teachers. These are Spirit-gifted people, who are called and raised up by God to equip other gifted people in the body of Christ.

As you begin your new church, you may have to serve in each of these five areas. However, one of your goals must be to develop other gifted leaders who will be raised up by God to lead the church with you.

1. Understanding the Five Roles[26]

Ministry vocation is a mixture of personal identity, God's calling, the Spirit's gifting, and community discernment. In *Ephesians 4*, we see genuine teamwork in action. I will refer to this teamwork-mix as APEST – the ministry of apostles, prophets, evangelists, shepherds and teachers. For there to be movement or growth in any context, a team should draw upon the natural energy and momentum that comes naturally in each member. Every person functions in unique ways. It is remarkable when a group allows each member to function out of their natural and supernatural capacities and gifts, thus contributing to the overall movement, direction, and wisdom of a team.

APEST Descriptions[27]

   A. Apostles – Missional Leaders and Movement Directors

   Apostles extend the Gospel. As the "sent ones," they ensure that the faith is transmitted from one context to another and from one generation to the next. They are always thinking about the future, bridging barriers, establishing the church in new contexts, developing leaders, networking trans-locally. Yes, if you focus solely on initiating new ideas and rapid expansion, you can leave people and organizations wounded. The shepherding and teaching functions are needed to ensure people are cared for rather than simply used.

   B. Prophets – Truth Proclaimers and Cultural Influencers

   Prophets know God's will. They are particularly attuned to God and His truth for today. They bring correction and challenge the dominant assumptions we inherit from the culture. They insist that the community obey what God has commanded. They question the status quo. Without the other types of leaders in place, prophets can become belligerent activists or, paradoxically, disengage from the imperfection of reality and become other-worldly.

   C. Evangelists – Gospel Presenters and Biblical Catalysts

   Evangelists recruit. These infectious communicators of the Gospel message recruit others to the cause. They call for a personal response to God's redemption in Christ, and also draw believers to engage the wider mission, growing the church. Evangelists can be so focused on reaching those outside the church that maturing and strengthening those inside is neglected.

   D. Shepherds – Pastoral Influencers and Caregivers

   Shepherds nurture and protect. As caregivers of the community, they focus on the protection and spiritual maturity of God's flock, cultivating a loving and spiritually mature network of relationships, making and developing disciples. Shepherds can value stability to the detriment of the mission. They may also foster an unhealthy dependence between the church and themselves.

E. Teachers – Communicators of Systematic, Biblical Truth

Teachers understand and explain. Communicators of God's truth and wisdom, they help others remain Biblically grounded to better discern God's will, guiding others toward wisdom, helping the community remain faithful to Christ's Word, and constructing a transferable doctrine. Without the input of the other functions, teachers can fall into dogmatism or dry intellectualism. They may fail to see the personal or missional aspects of the church's ministry.

2. Developing Others into Leaders

Let's assume you are starting a church by yourself. Everyone around you is either a very young Christian or perhaps not even a believer yet. Where are these leaders going to come from? You must develop them from within your church. How do you do that? More will be said about the discipleship process later in this book, but let me give you two major principles here that I believe will help you get started.

A. Develop them according to their gifts and uniqueness. Not all are evangelists. Not everyone will be an apostle. Not all have the spiritual gift of pastoring. Few may be prophets and not all will be teachers. This is where you must lead with discernment and help develop each of your leaders into the people God wants them to be.

B. You must be a developer of leaders. Don't do everything yourself. Teach and train others to do the ministry so that it will expand the way God wants it to.
- Follow this pattern: *Watch one, do one, teach one.* That means, first of all, *watch one.* Learn ministry skills yourself. Watch someone else do a particular ministry skill. In fact, watch more than one person! In your training with TTI, you are having great opportunities to watch and learn from experienced leaders. Second, *do one.* Practice and perform that skill, whether it is presenting the Gospel, preaching, counseling, discipling, etc. Finally, *teach one.* Teach one person one skill. Ultimately you will teach many people many skills.
- Learn this lesson: *Your greatest contribution in ministry will not be the things you accomplish, but it will be the things your disciples accomplish.* Too many pastors and church planters fall into the prideful trap of wanting to be known for their accomplishments: building a big church, preaching to many people, even writing many books. However, the greatest thing you can do is to build leaders. The Apostle John said: *I have no greater joy than to hear that my children* (referring to his spiritual children, those he discipled) *walk in truth* (3 John 4).
- Assume these roles:
  ▶ You are a coach. A coach is responsible for getting a team of players ready to play the game. The coach coaches; the players play. Give

your players experience "on the field." How are your young leaders getting the experience they need?
- You are also a trainer. A trainer imparts skills to those he is training. What skills are you imparting to your team of young leaders? How well are they learning those skills?
- Finally, you are a guide. A guide shows people the right path. Do you know where you are going? Does your team know where you are going? How are you taking them to where you want them to be?

Assignment:

Answer each of the questions in the section "Assume these roles" and assess how you are doing in your job of developing leaders in your church plant.

Chapter 6
What Does a Healthy Church Look Like?[28]

Introduction

How do you measure a church? Usually, people in certain parts of the world do it by numbers: *How many people attend each week? How large is your budget or how many people are giving? How big are your buildings, or how many buildings do you have?*

Such measuring is not always wrong – there is value in all of these. But the problem is that they often measure the wrong things…things that God doesn't necessarily measure when He evaluates a church.

As you meet in a home, under a tree, in a building, or wherever you gather, please learn to view the health of your church differently. As your church grows we want you to view it much more than the above.

So how does *God* measure a church? What does He care about? What are His values? As I was studying the book of *Ephesians* a few years ago, I saw something in Scripture that gave me a clue as to what God measures.

> *Ephesians 1:15-18 – Therefore I also, after I heard of your **faith** in the Lord Jesus and your **love** for all the saints, do not cease to give thanks for you, making mention of you in my prayers, that the God of our Lord Jesus Christ, the Father of glory, may give to you the spirit of wisdom and revelation in the knowledge of Him, the eyes of your understanding being enlightened, that you may know what is the **hope** of His calling, what are the riches of the glory of His inheritance in the saints.*

There were three words that impacted me after reading those verses: *faith, hope and love*. I have placed them in **bold** letters in the above quotation. I quickly realized that this was not the first time I'd heard those words used together. In fact, in most of Paul's letters and often in other New Testament epistles, those same three words are used:

> *1 Thessalonians 1:2-3 – We give thanks to God always for you all, making mention of you in our prayers, remembering without ceasing your work of **faith**, labor of **love**, and patience of **hope** in our Lord Jesus Christ in the sight of our God and Father.*

> *2 Thessalonians 1:3-4 – We are bound to thank God always for you, brethren, as it is fitting, because your **faith** grows exceedingly, and the **love** of every one of you abounds toward each other, so that we ourselves boast of you among the churches of God for your patience and **faith** in all your persecutions and tribulations that you endure.*

*Colossians 1:3-5 – We give thanks to the God and Father of our Lord Jesus Christ, praying always for you, since we heard of your **faith** in Christ Jesus and of your **love** for all the saints, because of the **hope** which is laid up for you in heaven, of which you heard before in the word of the truth of the Gospel.*

*1 Timothy 1:5 – Now the purpose of the commandment is **love** from a pure heart, from a good conscience and from a sincere **faith**.*

*1 Corinthians 13:13 – And now abide **faith, hope** and **love**. But the greatest of these is **love**.*

*1 Peter 1:20-22 – He indeed was foreordained before the foundation of the world, but was manifest in these last times for you who through Him believe in God who raised Him from the dead and gave Him glory, so that your **faith** and **hope** are in God. Since you have purified your souls in obeying the truth through the Spirit in sincere **love** of the brethren, **love** one another fervently with a pure heart.*

God measures a church, not by its size, its budget or if it has a building or not. God measures a church by its *faith, hope* and *love*. Let me define those briefly for you.

1. Faith is the Revelational Aspect

Do we believe God? Do we trust, obey and teach His Word? Are we committed to truth?

2. Love is the Relational Aspect

Do we love one another? Are we growing in community? Do we care for each other Biblically?

3. Hope is the Missional Aspect

Are we offering the Gospel as the hope of the world? Are we planting Bible-believing churches that will spread the Gospel?

When we talk about the values and qualities we want to see developed in churches, they ought to be values that can be clearly seen from God's Word. This chart will help amplify some of the distinctions in these three categories.

Faith	Love	Hope
Trusting God's Word	Reflecting God's Character	Participating in God's Mission
Our relationship to the Bible	Our relationship to Believers	Our relationship to Unbelievers
Key: knowing the Word	Key: selfless giving and sacrifice	Key: vision, impact, evangelism
Rooted in the Past	Grounded in the Present	Directed toward the Future
Christ's Work of Redemption	Christ's Sacrifice of Love	Christ's Promised Return
Great Commandment *Part 1*	Great Commandment *Part 2*	Great Commission

NOTES

When Linda and I were raising our three young children, we never told them, *GROW*! We concentrated on them being healthy: Were they eating right? Were they getting enough sleep? Were they free from illness and infections? Were they exercising properly? If all those things were present, we assumed they would grow. In the same way, when Paul measured a church, he did so by a rubric of three values: faith, hope and love. A church that is strong in each of those areas would be a healthy church... and a healthy church will be a growing and fruit-bearing church.

> **Assignment:**
>
> Evaluate your church plant by using the criteria of "faith, hope and love." If you have not yet planted a church, choose a church you know of or are involved with. How do they measure up? Write down your thoughts.

Chapter 7
God Wrote a Book on Church Planting

1. Introduction[29]

I believe that the most effective means for reaching people today is the planting of new, dynamic, Bible centered, Spirit filled churches. People are literally dying for a good healthy church. Dr. Bill Bright, the late founder of Campus Crusade for Christ, has said that in his over *60* years of evangelistic experience, he has found that more than *40%* of all people will respond positively to the Gospel if given a chance.[30] God is preparing hearts all over the world for the Good News of Jesus Christ being presented through the planting and establishing of healthy Word and Spirit balanced churches.

My experience of being a teaching pastor, planting a growing church, and consulting with Grace Global Network where we have partnered to plant thousands of churches around the world has taught me that the closer we follow the Bible and the Spirit in our church planting, the closer we get to God's model. And the more we do that, the more successful these churches will be.

I have read most of the literature that relates to church planting and I like most of it. I like the innovation and creativity of these different systems. I have used bits and pieces from many of these thoughtful leaders. But the more I study and experience successful and unsuccessful church plants, the more I am drawn back to the Biblical model found in the New Testament. The Bible has provided us with a Church Planting Manual that is better than any book I have ever read on the subject. God has not only given us a book on the subject, He has provided statistics and results the world has rarely seen.

What would you say to a Church Planting Manual that talks about a church being planted that grew from zero to *3,000* in one day? Interested? I am.

What about a church that quickly grew to *8,000* members in one month? What about that same church being able to develop a leadership team from the new converts that carried most of the administrative responsibilities so that the apostolic leadership team could continue to focus on preaching, teaching, and prayer? What about a church in which people brought their personal belongings to the leadership and asked how they could sacrificially give in order to build up the Kingdom of God? Those things are not in any church planting books I have read recently!

It can be done – but only by following the Biblical model. The plan is over *2,000* years old. It worked then and it still works today. The problem is not with the plan; the problem is with faith in the God of the plan.

God sent His Son to this earth because He passionately loves His creation. God gave us the best model for reaching people with the Kingdom of God-the local church. God knows how to plant powerful and successful churches. He has even written a book about it.

NOTES

God's Church Planting Manual is found in the book of *Acts* in the New Testament. After consulting with many church planters over the years and working with some of the most strategic thinkers of our time, I can honestly say that the book of Acts is the best book ever written on church planting.

The *Acts* of the Apostles, the fifth book of the New Testament, is strategically placed just after the Gospels. The Gospels teach us about Jesus. They introduce us to the Messiah. But it is primarily after that conversion to Christ that the power of the Holy Spirit begins to work in our lives. The *Acts* of the Spirit follow conversion.

The first thing we notice in *Acts* is the simultaneous work of the Spirit in reaching vast numbers of people for Christ and at the same time, the planting of a vital church. The entire book of *Acts* is a record of God's work in expanding the Kingdom of God through leaders who plant effective churches.

2. Background to the Book of *Acts*

A. Who wrote *Acts*?

Acts was written by Luke. He is the same author of the third Gospel. Luke was a Gentile believer from Antioch of Pisidia. He was a medical doctor according to Paul in *Colossians 4:14*. *Acts* contains specific language that shows Luke's medical knowledge. Luke was also a world-class historian and used his skills to investigate everything carefully as he began to write *Acts*. Luke was also a missionary, accompanying Paul on several parts of his missionary journeys. *Acts* was written during the early *AD 60's*, less than thirty years after Jesus' death in Jerusalem.

B. Why did Luke write *Acts*?

Luke's first book, the Gospel of *Luke*, told about the life of Jesus. *Acts* serves as a follow-up to that book, and talks about the birth and growth of the first century Church.

Dr. Luke begins the book of *Acts* where he left off in his Gospel account. *Acts* records the initial fulfillment of the Great Commission of *Matthew 28:18-20* as it traces the beginning and growth of the New Testament church. Christ's last words before His ascension were so perfectly realized in the Book of *Acts* that they effectively and concisely outline its contents: *You shall be My witnesses in Jerusalem (chapters 1-7), and in all Judea and Samaria (chapters 8-12) and even to the end of the earth (chapters 13-28)*. Thus, *Acts* traces the rapid expansion of the Gospel, beginning in Jerusalem and spreading throughout the Roman Empire.

C. To whom was it written?

Both the Gospel of *Luke* and the book of *Acts* were written to a man named Theophilus. His name means one *who is loved by God*. We know very little about this man, but it is likely that Theophilus was a Greek leader who became a Christian. Theophilus may have also given very generously of his finances to pay for Luke's travels and research.

D. What should I look for as I read the book of *Acts*?
- Evangelism
- Leadership Development
- The Role of the Holy Spirit
- Prayer
- The Power of God at work
- The Preaching of the Gospel
- The Planting of Churches

Assignment:

Read *Luke 1:1-4* and *Acts 1:1-4*. What do you learn about Luke, Theophilus, and these two books?

3. Structure of the Book of *Acts*

The book of *Acts* is centered around two main leaders. The *first twelve* chapters of *Acts* are mostly about Peter's ministry, primarily to Jewish believers. The remaining chapters, *13-28*, focus on Paul's ministry to the various cities and cultures throughout Asia Minor, taking the Gospel to the Gentiles (non-Jewish believers).

Acts is also structured geographically.
- The first *7 chapters* occur in Jerusalem.
- *Chapters 8-12* see the Gospel expand to the surrounding areas of Judea and Samaria.
- The remainder of Acts, *chapters 13-28*, records the Gospel moving to the whole world, with *chapter 28* ending in Rome, with Paul still planning to go on to Spain.

The following chart will help you visualize the structure of *Acts*.[31]

Witness in Jerusalem 1:1 — 8:4		Witness in Judea/Samaria 8:5 — 12:25	Witness to the Ends of the Earth 13:1 — 28:31	
Power of the Church 1:1 — 2:47	Progress of the Church 3:1 — 8:4	The Expansion of the Church 8:5 — 12:25	Paul's Three Journeys 13:1 — 21:16	Paul's Three Trials 21:17 — 28:31
Jews		Samaritans	Gentiles	
Peter		Philip	Paul	
2 Years (A.D. 33-35)		13 Years (A.D. 35-48)	14 Years (A.D. 48-62)	

NOTES

Assignment:

Beginning in the next chapter, you will be guided through the book of *Acts*. *Chapters 6-8* include a *mini-commentary* on this great book. It records the beginning of the Church, and how Christianity spread throughout the then-known-world. Begin reading *Acts* now – and record questions you have as you are reading below:

Chapter 8
The Acts of the Church Planters
Part One: Beginning in Jerusalem – Acts 1-7

Introduction

The book of *Acts* could be titled several different ways. The official title is *The Acts of the Apostles*, because it certainly records the early actions of Peter and all of Paul's three missionary journeys. It could also be titled *The Acts of the Holy Spirit*, because it was the Spirit who empowered all of the actions recorded in this wonderful book (*1:8*). In this section, I have chosen to call it *The Acts of the Church Planters*, because church planting is its primary focus, especially in *chapters 13-28*.

Jesus said in *Matthew 16:18*, *I will build My church, and the gates of Hell will not prevail against it.* Before Jesus ascended back to heaven, He commanded His followers to make disciples of all the nations (*Luke 24:46-49*). As seen earlier, Luke begins *Acts* with a summary of that commission and a description of how it would be carried out (*1:8*).

In the following chapters of this workbook I will lead you through an introduction to the book of *Acts*.[32] This will by no means be an exhaustive study of the book. But it will introduce you to its major themes, characters, stories and lessons.

- *Chapter 8* will cover *Acts 1-7*, the Church's beginnings in Jerusalem.
- *Chapter 9* will cover *Acts 8-12*, the Church's expansion to Judea and Samaria.
- *Chapter 10* will cover Acts 13-28, the Church's outreach to the ends of the earth.

As we go through each chapter in the book of *Acts*, I will first point out the content in each paragraph in that chapter, and then I will list some lessons for our lives. Though there will be *no assignments* in this section, take each of the lessons to heart... they will form your actions steps in response to the truths of this chapter.

1. *Acts 1:1-26*

A. *Chapter one* contains four separate paragraphs:
- *1:1-8* – <u>Jesus prepares the disciples for Pentecost</u>. It may be said that all of *Acts 1* relates to the preparation of the disciples for the coming of the Holy Spirit and the ministry they would have through their spiritual empowerment. In *verse 8* He gave them a promise of power (the coming of the Spirit), and a ministry strategy (expansion and multiplication) that would begin on the day of Pentecost. *Acts 1:3* and *1 Corinthians 15:1-7* tell us that Jesus appeared to them over a period of forty days, and spoke to them about things pertaining to the Kingdom of God (*1:3*).

- *1:9-11* – <u>Jesus ascends to heaven</u>. Though Jesus had told them He was returning to heaven, He promised He would not leave them as orphans (*Acts 1:5* cf. *John 14:18; 14:26; 15:26; Matthew 28:20; Luke 24:49*). He would send the Holy Spirit to comfort, teach, empower and lead their lives and ministry, and ultimately one day He would return from heaven in exactly the same way as they saw Him go into heaven (physically, bodily, and visibly).
- *1:12-14* – <u>The disciples gather to pray for the coming of the Holy Spirit</u>. Waiting on God and prayer are closely related in several places in the Old Testament, and therefore it is likely that they were praying constantly that the promised Spirit would descend. *Verse 14* tells us that they were *in one accord*. There was unity of purpose and unity of direction among the early Church.
  - ▶ Not only were the eleven remaining disciples present, but so were members of Jesus' family. Jesus had four brothers: James, Joseph, Judas (not to be confused with Judas Iscariot) and Simon (*Mark 6:3*). Apparently His post-resurrection appearances had convinced them that He was God (*1 Corinthians 15:7*). Also present were the women who ministered to Jesus and His followers (see *Luke 8:2-3*). They had accompanied them from Galilee (*Luke 23:55*), and witnessed the crucifixion and empty tomb (*Luke 23:49, 55-56; 24:2-11*). The total number of people in the upper room was about 120 (*1:15*).
- *1:15-26* – <u>The selection of Matthias to replace Judas</u>. Two men, Joseph and Matthias, met the necessary requirements to be considered for apostleship. The group turned the matter over *to the Lord* (*v. 24*), praying that He would make His choice known. *The lot*s were marked stones that were placed in a pot and then shaken out (See *1 Chronicles 26:13-16*). This does not imply that people should cast lots to make their decisions today, for there is no such command in any New Testament letter or Jesus' earthly teachings. The appointment of a twelfth apostle was a unique situation, a choice that was made by Jesus Himself. In the rest of the New Testament, the elders and deacons and other church leaders are chosen according to decisions made by human beings, whether by an apostle or by other leaders in the churches (See *Acts 6:3-6; 14:23; 15:22; 2 Cor. 8:19; 1 Tim 3:1-13; Titus 1:5-9*).

B. Lessons from *Acts 1*:
- <u>The importance of the Holy Spirit for us today</u> - Jesus has told His disciples that the key to life-empowerment and ministry-empowerment is the filling of the Holy Spirit. *Ephesians 5:18* tells us *Do not be drunk with wine...but be filled with the Spirit*. The Spirit's enabling power is marked by a joyful lifestyle (*John 15:11*) and the fruit of the Spirit (*Gal 5:22-23*).
- <u>The importance of prayer in Church Planting</u> - Prayer should not only be a regular part of each believer's life, it should be a central part of the life of the church as well.
- <u>The importance of developing new leadership</u> - As your church grows and develops; you will need to have new leaders. Begin to pray now for God to show you the people that He will raise up to have various positions of leadership in your church.

2. *Acts 2:1-47*

A. *Chapter 2* contains three distinct sections:
- *2:1-13* – <u>The Spirit descends at Pentecost</u>. The promise of the Spirit (cf. *Acts 1:5; Joel 2:28-32; Matthew 3:11*) is fulfilled at the feast of Pentecost. Pentecost was the second of the annual Jewish harvest festivals, coming 50 days after Passover. There are two parts to this narrative: the coming of the Spirit on believers (*2:1-4*) and the reaction of the Jewish crowd to the Spirit-filled Christians (*v. 5-13*).
- *2:14-41* – <u>Peter preaches at Pentecost</u>. Beginning with Peter's sermon and continuing through *chapter 5*, the witness of the Christians is confined to the city of Jerusalem and restricted to Jews. Peter's sermon consists primarily of Scriptural proofs:
    - *v. 14-21* interprets the miracle of tongues as a fulfillment of *Joel 2:28-32*.
    - *v. 22-36* presents Jesus as Messiah in fulfillment of *Ps. 16:8-11* and *110:1*.
    - *v. 37-41* concludes the sermon with a call to repentance and baptism, including an allusion to *Ps 132:10* and *2 Samuel 7:6-16*. His audience is convicted of their sin, and three thousand people are baptized and added to the church.
- *2:42-47* – <u>The new Christian community begins to take shape as a church</u>. This passage describes a number of activities characteristic of the earliest church, which are also prescriptive of what current churches should focus on:
    - The Apostle's teaching – (see *Acts 20:27-31; 2 Timothy 4:1-5*). These passages stress the necessity of sound doctrine and clear Biblical teaching that are necessary for a church to grow.
    - Fellowship – (see *Acts 4:32-35; Hebrews 10:24-25*). A truly Biblical church will be marked by people encouraging one another and building each other up in the Lord.
    - The Breaking of bread – *1 Corinthians 11:23-26*. This does not refer to eating meals together, though that is an important part of community. Rather, this specifically refers to celebrating The Lord's Supper together. There was a regular time of worship in their community experience, and an important part of that was remembering and celebrating the Lord's death on the cross for them.
    - Prayer – (see *Acts 3:1; 4:31; 12:5*). Prayer was a natural result of their desire to see God glorified in their lives and in the new Christian church, as well as to express their dependency upon Him.
    - Generosity and service – (see *Acts 4:32-37*). Because of their joy in the Lord and their love for other people, the early church generously gave to people in need and served them as unto the Lord.
    - Evangelism and outreach – (see *Acts 3:11-26; 4:8-20*). The new believers were infused with power and boldness, and they kept proclaiming the Gospel, even in the midst of much persecution. They could not stop speaking about what they had seen and heard (*4:20*).

B. Lessons from *Acts 2*
- <u>The early church stayed *on purpose*</u>. They knew what God had called them to do. Outreach, worship, fellowship, discipleship and service were essential elements of the church for them.
- <u>The early church had *power*</u>. Power in the New Testament is always associated with:
    ▶ The Holy Spirit – *Acts 1:8; 2:2*.
    ▶ Prayer – *Acts 1:14; 3:1*.
    ▶ Evangelism – *Acts 4:13, 20*.
- The Holy Spirit comes upon the believers in *verses 1-11* and they begin speaking in languages that were previously unknown to them. But the crowd that is gathered at the Jewish feast of Pentecost understood those languages. They heard them, each in their own dialect, proclaim the Gospel of God. This was one reason so many responded to the Gospel in *verse 41*.
- <u>This passage does not teach that the evidence of the Holy Spirit coming upon someone is speaking in tongues</u>. All believers are given one or more spiritual gifts, but not all believers speak in tongues (see *1 Cor. 12:30*). The evidence of the Holy Spirit is a changed life (*Gal 5:22-23*) and the belief that Jesus is Lord (*1 Cor. 12:3*).
- Peter preached a Spirit-empowered sermon that saw great fruit. How did Peter use his gift of evangelism?
    ▶ He began where they were in their understanding of Jesus. He told them that Jesus had been presented to them with miracles, wonders and signs which God performed through Him in their midst, *just as they themselves knew*.
    ▶ He used the Bible in his preaching. The Word of God is sharper than a two-edged sword (*Heb 4:12*) and is powerful to convict people of their sin (*Joh. 16:8-11*). In order to use the Bible effectively, it was obvious that Peter had spent much time in study.
    ▶ He talked about Jesus. There 32 references to Jesus in these 23 verses.
    ▶ His goal was to prove to them that Jesus was the promised Messiah. To a Jewish audience, that is what they needed to hear.
    ▶ He showed them their sin. In *verses 23* and *36*, he points out that *they* were the ones who crucified this Messiah.
    ▶ He promised them what would happen if they believed (*v. 38-40*). Their sins would be forgiven, they would receive the gift of the Holy Spirit, just as the Apostles had earlier, and they would be saved from God's wrath.
    ▶ He preached for decisions. He called them to a point where they had to make a choice about Jesus (*v. 40*). True preaching always brings men and women to the point where they must choose to believe in Jesus or reject Him.
- *Acts 2:38* <u>does not teach that baptism is required for salvation</u>. While baptism is important as the sign that one has been justified by faith and as the public declaration of one's faith in Christ and membership in a local body of believers, it is not the means of forgiveness of sins. The Bible is very clear that we are saved by grace alone through faith alone in Christ alone (*John 1:12; John 3:16; Acts 16:31; Romans 3:21-30; Romans 4:5; Romans 10:9-10; Ephesians 2:8-10; Philippians 3:9; Galatians 2:16*).

- Also in *verse 38*, *you will receive the gift of the Holy Spirit* does not mean some specific spiritual gift such as those listed in *1 Corinthians 12-14*. In this case, the gift is the Spirit Himself, coming to live and dwell within the life of the believer.

3. Acts 3:1-26

A. *Chapter 3* had two major paragraphs:
- *3:1-10* – The Healing of the Lame Beggar near the temple. This is the first example of an apostolic miracle, and attracts a crowd to hear Peter's second sermon in the temple area. In *Acts*, actions often lead to an explanation of what God is doing. Word and deed go together. Peter acknowledges that he does not have money to give to the lame beggar, but he has something far better: *Silver and gold I do not have, but what I do have I give you: In the name of Jesus Christ of Nazareth, rise up and walk* (Acts 3:6).
    - ▶ There are many supernatural events recorded in the book of *Acts*. Three words are used to describe those events: *miracle* tells us the description of the event and emphasizes that it is God's work, not the work of men; *wonder* describes the response to the event – people are amazed, convicted, and brought to the realization that God has visited them; *sign* is the word used to describe the meaning of the event. These miraculous events always point to the Deity of Jesus and the truthfulness of the Apostle's preaching.
- *3:11-26* – Peter's second evangelistic sermon. As with his first sermon, this one takes place inside the temple grounds. While Peter's sermon in *Acts 2* emphasized the fact that Jesus was their Messiah, this sermon is primarily a call for Jews to repent of their rejection of Jesus and focuses on the argument from Scripture.

B. Lessons from *Acts 3*

There are many lessons we can learn from the example of Peter and John.
- Peter and John were obeying God by going to worship in the temple (*v. 1*).
- The man had a need and was begging for money (*v. 2*).
- Peter and John were responsive to the situation (*v. 3*). They did not ignore the need of the man that was right in front of them.
- They got his attention by saying, *Look at us!* (*v. 4*). Before you can effectively minister to people, you must gain their attention.
- They gave him the simple Gospel (*v. 6*). They knew they did not have money to give him, but they could give him a touch from God.
- There are some today who preach a distorted Gospel known as the *Health and Wealth Gospel*, also called the "Prosperity Gospel." They teach that any true believer should never be sick and always be wealthy financially. However, here the Apostles publicly acknowledge they don't have any money. Jesus Himself died without owning any earthly possessions except a coat, and many of the greatest church and spiritual leaders throughout history have been poor and without money or possessions. Pastors and church planters must be careful to not slip into this false Gospel. You must also learn to be content with the finances God has given you (*Phi. 4:12*).

NOTES

- The healing was not dependent on the man's faith (*v. 7-8*). It was purely something that Peter and John did through their apostolic gifting.
- The result was that this man began to stand, walk and praise God (*v. 8*). The true result of evangelism is always praise to God.
- The response of the people is wonder and amazement at what had happened to him (*v. 9-10*). More importantly, they wanted to learn more about the men who performed this miracle. *Verse 11* says they ran together to find Peter and John, and became an audience ready to hear the Gospel message.
- God's work starts at the edge of impossibility. The next time you say *it's impossible*, listen for laughter from heaven. God will be smiling!
- Peter's sermon starts at *3:11*, but the results of that sermon are described in *4:1-4*.
- Peter is not afraid to confront them with their sin. He describes how they refused to take Pilate's advice, asking for a murderer's release instead (see *Luke 23:13-25*).
- The reference to God's *servant* (*3:13*) recalls *Isa 52:13-53:12*, the greatest description of Messiah's sacrificial death for the sins of the people.
- Peter stressed the sovereignty of God in carrying out His plan, but did not excuse the responsibility of the Jews for rejecting their Messiah. The issue in this sermon was the sin of the people. As a preacher, you must not be afraid to proclaim God's truth about sin.
- Peter proclaimed the Gospel in the power of the Holy Spirit and left the results up to God. In *verse 26* he promises that the Messiah will bless them as they turn to Him from their wickedness.

4. *Acts 4:1-37*

   A. This chapter contains four sections:
   - *4:1-4* – Peter and John are arrested by the council. As Peter and John were speaking, the priests and the captain of the temple guard (second in rank to the Jewish High Priest) and the Sadducees came up to them. These were the Jewish leaders and they were very upset that Peter and John had talked about the resurrection of Jesus. Because of this, they put them in jail overnight. As a result of this sermon and the subsequent imprisonment of the preachers, five thousand more people believed in Jesus.
   - *4:5-22* – Peter and John defend themselves before the High Priest. Amidst the accusations by these powerful leaders, Peter and John were filled with the Spirit and demonstrated remarkable boldness, authority and conviction, and the ability to testify with wisdom and insight as Jesus had already promised them would happen (*Mat. 10:19-20; Luk. 12:11-12; 21:12-15*). They refused to back down on their commitment to telling others about Jesus.
   - *4:23-31* – The believers pray for boldness. Please notice that their prayers have real content and substance. They are not simply crying out *Help us!* Rather, they recognize God's sovereign character, and pray quoting Scriptural promises. They do not ask for relief from persecution, but rather for boldness to continue to speak in the midst of the threats of the people. The result of their prayer (*v. 31*), is that the building they were gathered in literally shook with God's power. God's Spirit filled them with power and authority and they continued to speak the Word of God with boldness.

- *4:32-37* – <u>The believers demonstrate uncommon generosity</u>. In the midst of persecution, true character always emerges. All the believers were of *one heart and soul*, and they generously gave everything they had to the continuing ministry of the church. All needs were met, and the grace of God was upon them all. In the midst of this, a future leader emerges. Joseph, a native of Cyprus, sells a large piece of land and donates it to the ministry. This Joseph, who is nicknamed *Barnabas* (which means Son of Encouragement), eventually becomes the one who mentors and encourages the greatest Church Planter of all time, the Apostle Paul.

B. Lessons from *Acts 4*
- How should we respond to opposition?
  - ▶ Be filled with the Holy Spirit (*v. 8*)
  - ▶ Be respectful. In *verse 8*, Peter addressed them by their religious titles.
  - ▶ Witness to the Person of Jesus Christ (*v. 9-10*). The issue is Jesus. Don't get focused to other issues.
  - ▶ Point to the evidence of a changed life (*v. 9-10*). Your testimony – or the testimony of others – is one of the most powerful arguments for the reality of Jesus.
  - ▶ Proclaim the Gospel clearly and with authority. Peter said, *There is salvation in no one else, for there is no other name under heaven given among men by which we must be saved* (*v. 12*).
  - ▶ Quote Scripture, as Peter did in *verse 11*.
  - ▶ Demonstrate an authentic boldness, confidence and authority (*v. 13*). As the Jewish leaders observed the boldness of Peter and John and perceived that they were uneducated, common men, they were astonished. They recognized them as having been with Jesus.
  - ▶ Refuse to compromise your convictions. The authorities had commanded them to stop talking about Jesus. Peter and John said they couldn't do that, because there was a higher authority (God) than them. The Apostles *could not stop talking about what they had seen and heard*. Can you say the same thing about your lifestyle?
- How to pray in the midst of opposition:
  - ▶ Pray with other Christians. Don't isolate yourself.
  - ▶ Claim the presence and authority of God over the situation – *Isaiah 40:15, 23-26; 41:10-11*.
- How can you create a spirit of generosity in your church?
  - ▶ Communicate that *it is not equal gifts, but equal sacrifice*. There are some who are blessed with financial riches who can give a lot. There are others who do not have many earthly possessions. Each person must be encouraged to be generous, regardless of their financial status.
  - ▶ Remember that people respond to encouragement rather than coercion. Do not force people to give by making them feel guilty. Rather, develop an environment where the vision of the church captivates people's hearts. In the long run, they will give far more with that as their motivation.
  - ▶ Lift up models of generosity (like Barnabas). Often those who are generous will become strong leaders in your church. As you teach on generosity, you must demonstrate generosity yourself. Practice what

NOTES

> **NOTES**

you preach! If you are not a generous giver, then how can you expect your followers to be generous?

5. Acts 5:1-42

A. *Chapter five* contains three paragraphs:
- *5:1-11* – <u>Ananias and Sapphira lie to the leadership of the church</u>. The positive picture of the community's sharing (and specifically recognizing Barnabas for his generosity) is stained by the account of a couple who abused the practice of giving by holding back a portion of the gift while claiming to be giving it totally to the church. Ananias and Sapphira were under no obligation to give all their proceeds to the church. Their sin was not in limiting the amount of their gift, but it was in claiming that they gave it all. Their selfishness was influenced by Satan, who had *filled their hearts* to lie to the Holy Spirit. They ultimately paid for their sin with their lives.
  - ▶ The context is important to note: this event comes in between references to the Spirit's power (*4:31, 33; 5:12-16*). The Spirit was closely linked to the unity of the fellowship manifested in their sharing. Ananias and Sapphira abused the fellowship through their deception and thereby threatened its unity. They were believers who lived a lie from the enemy before their brothers and sisters in Christ. Christians still sadly do this today.
- *5:12-16* – <u>Many signs and wonders were done among the people by the hands of the Apostles</u>. The Christians had prayed for God to grant them power to perform *signs and wonders* (*4:30*). This was mightily fulfilled through the Apostles.
- *5:17-42* – <u>The Apostles are again brought before the Council, are imprisoned and ultimately released</u>. The lone voice in the Sanhedrin (the Jewish law court) to speak against an immediate death sentence for the Apostles was *Gamaliel*. He was the most prominent rabbi of his day and the teacher of Paul (*22:3*). He was a Pharisee who had considerable influence in the Council.
  - ▶ Gamaliel cites two examples from Jewish history to support his basic argument that movements not backed by God always come to nothing. Both examples were failed movements, the first being that of a revolutionary named *Theudas*, and the second *Judas the Galilean* (*v. 37*).
  - ▶ The Council takes his advice, but beats and tortures the Apostles before they release them. *Verse 41* says that the Apostles *left the council, rejoicing that they were counted worthy to suffer dishonor for Jesus.*

B. Lessons from *Acts 5*
- Sin will always destroy the unity and mission of the Church. It must be dealt with. God has instituted policies for church discipline (*Matthew 18:15-20*) to maintain the purity of the fellowship.
- Most people will respond to godly leadership (like Barnabas) with humility and obedience. However, some will respond with pride and selfishness, wanting the attention and praise that leadership gives, but without the integrity necessary to be qualified for a leadership position in the church.

- If you encounter persecution because of your faith, respond the way the Apostles did. Rejoice that you are counted worthy to suffer dishonor for Jesus.

6. *Acts 6:1-15*

A. *Chapter six* contains two short paragraphs:
- *6:1-7* – <u>Seven qualified leaders are chosen to serve</u>. The numerical growth of the church created problems when a number of Hellenistic (Greek-speaking) Jews responded to the Gospel. The resulting language barrier led to the neglect of some needy widows, and the Apostles called upon the Greek-speaking community to choose leaders to meet the need. Though these servants were initially called to serve food to these widows, they still had to have excellent qualifications: *good reputation, full of the Spirit and wisdom*. Their ability to serve freed the Apostles to devote themselves to the ministry of the Word and prayer. The reality of disorganization and the sin of prejudice was now dealt with.
- *6:8-15* – <u>Stephen is arrested</u>. The Greek word for witness is the word *martyr*. Stephen becomes the ultimate witness as he becomes the first martyr of the early church. This paragraph describes his powerful character and ministry (*full of grace and power, doing great wonders and signs among the people, speaking with wisdom and Spirit-empowerment – v. 8, 10*), as well as his arrest on false accusations.

B. Lessons from *Acts 6*
- Two realities arise during times of ministry growth and blessing: complaints arise, and servants are needed. Don't be surprised when there are problems. Identify them, and challenge qualified men and women to help meet the need.
- Tackle disorganization and prejudice head on in your ministry. This will mean handing over some responsibilities to other qualified people.
- Maintain high standards for all who serve in your church. Character, integrity and spiritual maturity are essential, even for the unseen tasks.
- Real servants make themselves available to serve – *2 Timothy 2:4*.
- Real servants pay attention to needs – *Galatians 6:10; Proverbs 3:28*.
- Real servants do their best with what they have – *Ecc. 11:4*.
- Real servants approach every task with equal dedication – *Col. 3:23*.
- Real servants are faithful to their ministry – *Mat. 25:23*.
- Real servants maintain a low profile. They do not need public acknowledgement – *Mat. 6:1; 1 Peter 5:5*.
- Realize a dynamic servant will sometimes have a clear speaking gift. Stephen's speaking gift was so obvious and powerful that he was martyred for it. Also see Philip as a communicator in the book of *Acts*. Do not peg current or future deacons as people who cannot preach or teach.
- Serving in the church will qualify you for greater positions of leadership. The first martyr of the church got his start by serving food to widows.

NOTES

7. Acts 7:1-60

A. *Chapter seven* is one long sermon preached by Stephen prior to his martyrdom.
   - Stephen, speaking to a Jewish audience, traces the history of the Jews in the Old Testament. He discusses Abraham, Joseph, Moses, David, Solomon, and the Prophets. His message is that the Jews have always rejected God's leaders, and now they have made the ultimate rejection in crucifying Jesus.
   - This is not the trial of Stephen. It is the trial of the Jewish leaders, and they are found guilty as charged.
   - The intensity of persecution comes to its fullest intensity.
     ▶ *2:13* – they were mocked.
     ▶ *4:17, 21* – they were threatened.
     ▶ *5:18* – they were imprisoned.
     ▶ *5:40* – they were beaten physically.
     ▶ *7:58-60* – Stephen is murdered.
   - Notice the response of Jesus as Stephen enters heaven: He is standing – as if to honor Stephen. Jesus may still stand today to greet each of His martyrs.

B. Lessons from *Acts 7*
   - Notice the qualities of Stephen's response (*v. 59-60*): He asks God to *receive my spirit* and prays, *Do not hold this sin against them*. That is exactly the same response of Jesus as He was being crucified.
   - Notice the similarities between the trials of Jesus with the trial of Stephen:
     ▶ Both trials had lying witnesses who made false accusations.
     ▶ Both men prayed, *Father forgive them* and *do not hold this sin against them*.
     ▶ Jesus prayed, *Into Your hands I commit My Spirit*. Stephen prayed, *receive my spirit*.
     ▶ Both were killed outside the city, signifying rejection by the Jewish leadership.
   - Notice the results of Stephen's death:
     ▶ The Jewish nation was put on trial and officially declared guilty of crucifying Jesus and rejecting the Gospel.
     ▶ This precipitated the first wave of persecution against the church (*8:1-3*).
     ▶ It also caused the church to begin to scatter and move into the regions of Judea and Samaria.
   - Persecution will cause some to fall away. It will also cause others to courageously rise up and trust God for greater impact in the midst of the persecution. It has been said that *the blood of the martyrs is the seed that causes the church to grow. Yes, the blood of the martyrs is still the seed of the saints. We say in unison, come Lord Jesus.*

Chapter 9
The Acts of the Church Planters Part Two: Expanding to Judea and Samaria – Acts 8-12

Introduction

Our study in *Acts* continues, now moving into the second major section of the book. The Jews have officially rejected the Gospel of Jesus and killed Stephen the Evangelist. Now the church begins moving out of Jerusalem and into the surrounding regions.

1. Acts 8:1-40

A. *Chapter eight* contains two separate paragraphs:
- *8:1-3* – <u>Saul damages the church</u>. Saul fully approved of Stephen's execution. The believers were scattered all over Judea and Galilee, except for the Apostles who were able to stay in Jerusalem. Saul began to attack the church entering every home and taking the believers to prison. He becomes the major enemy of the church.
- *8:4-40* – <u>The church begins to minister to new regions</u>. Philip, another of the faithful servants from *Acts 6*, becomes an evangelist to Samaria and begins to see fruitful results in his preaching. Not only do many Samaritans believe, but so does Simon, a magician who claimed to be *The Great One*. Commentators differ over whether Simon had genuine saving faith. Peter's strong rebuke to Simon soon after his 'conversion' suggests that he did not have genuine saving faith (see *v. 20-21*). Philip is miraculously transported by the Holy Spirit into the desert region, to meet the Ethiopian Eunuch, a political leader whose heart had been prepared by the Holy Spirit. He is converted, baptized and sent on his way to Ethiopia, where church history tells us he was instrumental in planting churches.

B. Lessons from *Acts 8*
- God certainly seems to have a sense of humor. The most intense persecutor of the church (Saul) appears causing havoc on the ministry. But by the middle of the next chapter, Saul has been dramatically converted to Jesus and is well on his way to becoming known as the Apostle Paul.
- Boldly pray for your enemies. Pray for their salvation. Who knows what God might do!
- I sometimes wonder if the church had become comfortable in Jerusalem. They were commanded to go to the world, but seven chapters into the story they are still in the same city. God sent persecution and all of a sudden, they are forced to go in a new direction. God may have strange ways of accomplishing His will... but He sovereignly does so. Your possible persecution could be God moving you to another area to start a church planting center. Avoid being too comfortable.

NOTES

- Be wary of false conversions. Simon the magician wanted the *power* of the Gospel without repenting of his sins. Peter had the discernment to warn him strenuously (*v. 20*). Salvation is a free gift, but some do not accept it, they mock the free gift.
- Look for people whose hearts have been prepared by God's Spirit. It was obvious that the Ethiopian Eunuch was a God-fearer who simply needed to hear a simple explanation of the Gospel. God is always working…keep your eyes open for those who are ready to receive Christ.
- The greatest thing we have to offer God is to be completely available and dedicated to Him. Philip wound up in Samaria because of the persecution happening in Jerusalem and began preaching, and many responded. Then he is miraculously sent to the desert and begins a conversation with someone from Africa. It resulted in Christianity expanding to a new continent!

2. Acts 9:1-43

A. *Chapter nine* contains three paragraphs:
- *9:1-19* – <u>The conversion of Saul of Tarsus</u>. Saul's conversion may seem out of place, with the emphasis on this section being the church in Jerusalem, Judea and Samaria as led by Peter and certain Greek-speaking Jews like Stephen and Philip. But, it does fit into this time frame. Paul's conversion is related in detail three times in *Acts*: here in story form, and twice through Paul's testimony before a Jewish mob (*22:3-11*) and before King Agrippa II (*26:2-18*). Luke does not record the date of Paul's conversion, but a reasonable estimate is around *AD 33-34*.
- *9:20-31* – <u>Saul begins to preach Christ</u>. Immediately after his conversion, Saul begins witnessing in Damascus and Jerusalem. In *Galatians*, Paul records that during this time he *went away into Arabia and returned again to Damascus* (*Gal 1:17*). The pattern of Paul beginning his witness in the synagogues occurs throughout *Acts*, as does the pattern of opposition developing there (*9:23*). Saul targeted leaders.
- *9:32-43* – <u>A short summary of Peter's ministry</u>. Peter began to witness outside Jerusalem in the coastal plain of Judea, healing the lame Aeneas (*9:32-35*) and restoring life to Dorcas (*9:36-43*). God then led him to Caesarea to witness to a group of Gentiles.

B. Lessons from *Acts 9*
- Jesus asked Saul, *Why are you persecuting Me?* This shows His close identity with His followers. To persecute Christians was to persecute Jesus.
- Jesus appeared to a believer in Damascus (Ananias), instructing him to go to Saul. He was told to assist him in recovery of his sight, and inform him of his special calling. I can imagine this caused a great deal of anxiety in Ananias' heart: *"God, You want me to go WHERE? To speak to WHO? He's dangerous! He kills Christians – and I do not want to be his next victim!"* And yet Ananias obeyed. There are times in ministry where you must do things you are afraid of doing. But God will be with you. He will give you His peace. And as you look back on it later, you will be very glad you obeyed.

3. Acts 10:1-48

A. *Acts 10* is the story of Peter and Cornelius and how the Gospel finally went to a Gentile audience.
- Cornelius resided at Caesarea, a city on the coast 31 miles (50 km) north of Joppa. Caesarea was the seat of the Roman government of Judea. Cornelius was a *centurion*, a commander of *100* men and a member of the *Italian Cohort*, consisting of *600* men under the command of six centurions. Cornelius was socially important and wealthy.
- God spoke to Peter in a vision (*10:28*) that he was to go and present the Gospel of Jesus to a Gentile who lived nearby. That was a real step of faith for Peter, who, as a good Jew, would never set foot inside a Gentile's home. However, he knew God had spoken to him, and he obeyed.
- His message to the Gentiles is unique among the sermons of *Acts* in providing a summary of Jesus' ministry. It contains no scriptural proofs and was cut short before Peter could give an invitation to trust in Christ. It is quite likely that the speech was an extended one, of which Luke gives a shortened account.
- The Holy Spirit fell in a way that was visible and audible from the response of the people on whom he fell (*v. 44-46*). These Gentiles had come to genuine saving faith in Christ, and received the new covenant power and fullness of the Holy Spirit, which was a sign that they had been accepted by God as full and equal members of His people. The fact that they had not followed any Mosaic ceremonial laws (such as those concerning circumcision, sacrifice, and dietary restrictions) before receiving the gift of the Spirit is an important point, as soon becomes evident (see *11:15-17*).

B. Lessons from *Acts 10*
- God is at work graciously preparing our hearts to do what He wants. God knew it would be tough to convince Peter that he was supposed to preach to the Gentiles. He graciously prepared his heart by speaking to him in a vision. Peter obeyed – a sign of his growing maturity in the faith. The foundation is now laid for the Gospel going to the ends of the earth.
- Love the lost. Historically, Jews *hated* Gentiles. They despised them, thinking that they were not worth saving. And yet going back to the Abrahamic Covenant in the Old Testament (*Genesis 12*), the Jews were supposed to be a blessing to the whole world. Perhaps you are ministering in a situation where there is hatred and distrust among various people-groups. Your love for God – and His love for those people – must lead you beyond those cultural barriers to be able to share the Gospel with them.
- The Holy Spirit fell on these new believers in a way that was visible and audible from their response. These new Gentile believers spoke in tongues (*Acts 10:46*) just like the Jews did on the Day of Pentecost in *Acts 2:1-11*. Though speaking in tongues may occur where the Gospel penetrates a new culture for the first time, it is not usual that believers speak in tongues. In fact, Paul specifically said in *1 Corinthians 12:30* that not everyone speaks in tongues. As noted earlier, speaking in tongues is not a normal sign of the Holy Spirit falling on someone.

NOTES

- Water Baptism is a very important part of our Christian life. These new believers were baptized (*v. 40*) as a sign that they had been saved by Jesus. Baptism is one of two important ordinances of the church (the other is the Lord's Supper). You should regularly baptize new Christians soon after their conversion. However, be certain that they can give a credible profession of faith in Christ (a clear testimony of how they came to know Jesus as their Lord and Savior) before you baptize them.
- Peter remained in Cornelius' home for several days. This was more than simply an example of hospitality. Peter was beginning to disciple these new believers in the basics of the Christian faith.

4. *Acts 11:1-30*

A. *Chapter 11* contains two paragraphs:
  - *11:1-18* – <u>Peter reports to the church about the conversion of the Gentiles</u>. After Cornelius' conversion, Peter goes to Jerusalem, where some of Peter's fellow Jewish Christians questioned his acceptance of the Gentiles. Peter defended his action by retelling the events of the Gentile conversions with an emphasis on how God led him to Cornelius.
  - *11:19-30* – <u>The ministry of the church at Antioch</u>. The persecution that arose over Stephen (see *8:1, 4*) caused believers to be *scattered* and led to the spread of the Word among Jews in various outlying regions. The primary language of these areas was Greek. Antioch was the largest city of the area, and the capital of the Roman province of Syria, with a population of a half million or more. Only Rome and Alexandria were larger in ancient times. The Jewish Christians spoke the Word only to other Jews, because they had not yet heard about the events of *10:1-11:18*.
    ▶ The hand of the Lord was with these believers (*v. 21*) and many people came to faith in Jesus. The Church in Jerusalem sent Barnabas to Antioch to evaluate the situation. When he saw the grace of God at work, he rejoiced and encouraged them to remain faithful to the Lord. He also went to Tarsus to look for Saul (*v. 25*) and brought him to Antioch to help disciple these new believers.

B. Lessons from *Acts 11*
  - It is always good and proper to have godly leaders to whom you are accountable. Even Peter, the leader of the early Church, was accountable to his brothers in Jerusalem. When they heard about his experience in Caesarea, they called him to give an account of his actions. There will be times when your leaders ask you why you did certain things. Do not get defensive and angry about this. They are there to care for your soul and to protect you. Answer honestly, as Peter did, and point to how God led you in that situation.
  - Barnabas took a risk in going to Tarsus to look for Saul. Was Saul mature enough to come to Antioch and be one of the elders there? Did he have what it took to minister in a foreign culture? Would this *Pharisee of the Pharisees (Philippians 3:5)* be able to get past his Jewish heritage and minister to a congregation that was increasingly comprised of new Gentile believers? Barnabas took that risk because of Saul's growing reputation as a strong defender of the Christian faith. Learn to believe in people.

Give them opportunities to minister and serve. Like Barnabas, be a *Son of Encouragement* to others.
- Be secure to allow others God has called you to minister with exceed your work. Do not compare. Fulfill your mission.

5. *Acts 12:1-25*

A. There are three paragraphs in *chapter 12*:
- *Acts 12:1-5* – The Apostle James, John's brother, is killed and Peter imprisoned. King Herod executed the Apostle James and imprisoned Peter, intending to kill him also. This James is not to be confused with *James the brother of Jesus*, who was the author of the book of James and a prominent leader in the Jerusalem church.
- *Acts 12:6-19* – Peter is rescued. Peter was half asleep throughout his 'escape' from prison. The angel had to rouse him and direct him (*v. 7-8*) and he remained in a stupor until the angel led him through the gates and into a side street (*v. 9-11*).
- *Acts 12:20-25* – The death of Herod and the increasing ministry of the Church. *Chapter 12* begins and ends with Herod Agrippa I. The persecutor of the church now brings about his own death.

B. Lessons from *Acts 12*
- Suffer well. Jesus had predicted James' suffering (*Mark 10:39*). Perhaps this was a gracious way of Jesus saying, *James, you won't have long to serve me. Finish well!* You don't know when you will die. Perhaps you will live many, many years and faithfully serve Jesus. Perhaps, like James, you will have the honor of dying a martyr's death for your Savior. But since none of us knows when we will die, we must commit to living life to the fullest and serving Jesus in the greatest ways we can. Read *2 Timothy 4:1-8*.
- There is quite a bit of humor in the Bible. In this chapter, the early church must have been scared to death. James was killed. Peter was likely to be next. After that, Herod might come after all of them. And so they gathered to pray for Peter's release. God answered that prayer, and Peter shows up at the house, banging on the gates to be let in. Too involved in their prayer meeting to see what the noise was, they sent the servant girl Rhoda to deal with the problem. Rhoda recognizes Peter, but in her joy to tell the others, leaves Peter at the gates. When she goes back in, no one believers her. In fact, they come up with some strange response that what she saw was *Peter's ghost*. All this time, Peter is still banging away at the gates. Now that's a funny story. And aren't you glad that God is gracious and patient with all of us?
- When you pray in the character and name of Jesus Christ, expect Him to answer.

NOTES

Chapter 10
The Acts of the Church Planters Part Three: Reaching to the Ends of the Earth – Acts 13-28

Introduction

Our study in *Acts* continues, now moving into the third major section of the book. Saul/Paul has been converted to Christ and is ready to begin leading the missionary enterprise to the ends of the earth.

1. *Acts 13:1-52*

   A. *Chapter 13* contains four separate paragraphs:
   - *13:1-3* – <u>The Antioch Church commissions Barnabas and Saul</u>. The church in Antioch had already been proclaiming the Gospel to the Gentiles nearby, and Saul and Barnabas had participated (*11:19-26*). Now the Spirit led the church to send them on a wider mission, well beyond the borders of Syria.
   - *13:4-12* – <u>Barnabas and Saul witness in Cyprus</u>. The two missionaries worked first on the island of Cyprus, Barnabas' home (*4:36*). This first of Paul's three missionary journeys is narrated in *13:4-14:26*. It likely began in *AD 46* or *47* and lasted perhaps a year and a half.
   - *13:13-41* – <u>Paul preaches in the synagogue of Pisidian Antioch</u>. From Cyprus the missionaries sailed to the southern coast of what today is Turkey. Paul's sermon (*v. 16-41*) consisted of three parts: an overview of Old Testament history (*v. 16-25*), God's ultimate provision in Jesus Christ (*v. 26-37*), and an invitation (*v. 38-41*). Do you remember Stephen's sermon from *Acts 7*? This sermon is very similar in that it covers an overview of Israel's history. Both sermons emphasize God's raising up leaders for Israel, but with a major difference: Stephen pointed to Israel's rejection of its God-sent leaders, while Paul stressed God's grace in providing the leaders.
   - *13:42-52* – <u>Paul turns to the Gentiles</u>. Although the response at the synagogue was favorable, with Paul being asked to preach again, the Jews turned against him the next Sabbath when a large group of Gentiles showed up. Paul responded by turning to the Gentiles, a pattern he would continue in every city he visited: beginning with the Jews, then turning to the Gentiles when opposition forced him from the synagogue.

   B. Lessons from *Acts 13*
   - *Acts 13:1-3* lists five prophets and teachers in the Church at Antioch. Notice here – and in the rest of the book of *Acts* – that the leadership of a local church involves several people, not just one point leader. Plurality of leadership is the norm of the New Testament Church. It is fine for a church to start out with one leader. Often God calls a church planter to begin a

work by himself. But it is important that it not stay that way long. Begin to build other leaders. Give them opportunities to lead, teach and preach. Ultimately your greatest joy will be the reproduction of leaders in the life of your church.
- Intentionality and a plan are essential in reproducing leaders, including preachers and teachers. This insures quality, dynamic health and the lack of focus on one man. The team has a leader, but the influence is shared.
- What a great team of prophets and teachers the church at Antioch had! And yet when the Lord called them to send their two best to the mission field, they obeyed immediately. This is a great example to churches around the world that they are to be responsive to the leading of the Holy Spirit, and, when He calls, they must send their best.
- In the New Testament, the ordering of names is important. The primary leader is mentioned first, then the second-in-command, and then the others after that. When the missionary trip started, the names were *Barnabas and Saul/Paul*. But by the end of their first journey, it was Paul and Barnabas. What happened? Barnabas saw Paul's giftedness on display – and he willingly took a step back and let Paul take the lead. That required humility, security and a selflessness that is rarely found today. Will you be like Barnabas? One of my colleagues has as a life goal that those he trains will far surpass him in ministry fruitfulness. That's a real sign of a secure leader.

2. *Acts 14:1-28*

A. *Chapter 14* has three paragraphs:
- *14:1-7* – <u>Paul and Barnabas are rejected at Iconium</u>. Forced to leave Antioch, the two missionaries went to Iconium, where a great number of people believed. But even with the fruitful ministry, there was great opposition.
- *14:8-23* – <u>The two missionaries witness in Lystra</u>. Lystra was populated mainly by Gentiles and had no synagogue. The ministry of Paul and Barnabas centered around the healing of a lame man and the attempt of the people to worship them.
- *14:24-28* – <u>Paul and Barnabas return to Antioch in Syria</u>. Coming home after eighteen months "of travel," Paul and Barnabas give a report to the church about all that God accomplished through their efforts.

B. Lessons from *Acts 14*
- In *14:1*, both Paul and Barnabas are referred to as Apostles (*v. 4, 14*). The word carries the general meaning of *one who is sent* but it is often used throughout the New Testament in a more technical term for someone specifically chosen and commissioned by Christ for the proclamation of the Gospel, as in the case of the original twelve Apostles (e.g., *Matt 10:2; Mark 3:14; Luke 9:1; Acts 1:2, 15-26*). The Apostle Paul understood his calling as an apostle to be comparable to the calling of the original Twelve in this technical sense. This was one who had seen Christ and who had been specifically chosen and appointed by Christ. This was based on the fact that Paul, on the road to Damascus, had in fact personally seen the risen Christ and had been chosen by Him (*26:16-17*) to proclaim the Gos-

NOTES

pel to the Gentiles. Commentators differ as to whether the word *apostles* here in *Acts 14:4* and *14* refers to Paul and Barnabas as being apostles in the same technical sense as the original Twelve, or whether this is intended in the general sense of *ones who are sent* (cf. *13:2-3*), where Paul and Barnabas are *set apart* by the Holy Spirit and *sent off* by the church in Antioch. A look at *Galatians* and *2 Timothy* makes it clear that Paul was like the original Twelve. The bottom line is this: are you sent by God? To whom are you sent?

- *Acts 14:22-23* contains a great summary of Church Planting. Paul and Barnabas spent their time: *strengthening the souls of the disciples, exhorting them to continue in the faith, and saying, "We must through many tribulations enter the Kingdom of God." So when they had appointed elders in every church and prayed with fasting, they commended them to the Lord in whom they had believed.* In this passage you see the need for pouring your life into men so they will become solid leaders in your church.

- Also notice from *14:22-23* that it was important for Paul and Barnabas to appoint godly leaders (elders) in every church. Notice two important qualifications: they were appointed by men with spiritual discernment (in this case, Paul and Barnabas) and there were at least two elders in every situation. Whenever possible, do not leave a new church in the hands of just one person. Where there are several leaders, there is accountability and teamwork.

- In *14:24-28*, Paul and Barnabas retraced their steps and sailed back to Antioch. There they gave an extended missions report. It is important for us to report back to the people who have prayed for us and financially supported us, giving reports about all that God has done. Paul and Barnabas spent a long time with the disciples there. They needed refreshment, encouragement and the community that their friends and loved ones gave them.

3. Acts 15:1-41

A. *Chapter 15* contains two very important paragraphs:
- 15:1-35 – <u>The Council at Jerusalem</u>. A conference was held in Jerusalem (around *AD 48* or *49*) to discuss conditions for Gentile membership in the church. The issue was raised by the strict Pharisaic wing of the Jerusalem church (*v. 1-5*). The Gentile mission was defended by Peter (*v. 6-11*). A solution was proposed by James (*v. 12-21*), and an official agreement was reached (*v. 22-35*). The fact that James is key to the resolution shows that the Jewish and Gentile believers were less divided than some try to make them. Those who complained here were on the fringe of the church, and their hard line view was rejected.
  - ▶ The Antioch church had reached out to many Gentiles (*11:20-21*), and God had given Paul and Barnabas great success among the Gentiles on their mission (*14:27*). No evidence exists that these Gentiles had been circumcised or required to live by the Mosaic law. In fact, the Spirit had come on them without such an act, as Peter will argue. Some conservative Jewish Christians argued that Gentiles should undergo these things since they were required of all converts to Judaism. The issue was whether Gentiles needed to become Jews, and follow Jewish ceremonial laws in order to become Christians.

- ▶ James agreed with Peter that they should not trouble the Gentiles with the ritual laws. But he knew that Gentile Christians would have contact with Jewish Christians who still kept the ceremonial provisions, including laws about sacrifices, festivals, unclean foods, and circumcision. He offered a proposal by which Gentile Christians could have fellowship with Jewish Christians and avoid giving unnecessary offense. This proposal was agreed on by the early church.
- *15:36-41* – The argument at the beginning of the Second Missionary Journey. Before setting out on his new mission, Paul asked Barnabas to accompany him. A sharp disagreement arose between them over whether to take Mark. Paul and Barnabas differed over whether John Mark should be allowed to go with them on this mission, since he had deserted them earlier on the first journey. Barnabas felt allegiance to the *man*, and he saw the potential for great things in John Mark. Paul felt allegiance to the *mission*, and he did not want the cause of Christ to suffer because of John Mark's lack of commitment. In the end, Barnabas took Mark on a separate mission and Paul chose Silas to be his companion. Neither was wrong, both fulfilled their unique calling.

B. Lessons from *Acts 15*
- We can learn much from the way the early Church handled the Gentile controversy. They did so properly, in order, and without allowing emotions to get in the way. In this account, you see the respect for Church leadership that Paul and Barnabas had. The leaders in Jerusalem also acted maturely by listening carefully to the missionaries' account, not misusing their power, and seeking God's wisdom to discern what to do. There will be times in your ministry that you must make hard decisions. Don't act in haste. Get all the facts, and prayerfully seek God's will.
- I've heard many different opinions about Paul and Barnabas' argument over John Mark's worthiness to participate in the mission. I've come to this conclusion: they were both right. Barnabas saw through Mark's previous desertion and knew he would be a fruitful leader for many years to come. He knew that if they did not include Mark, he would become discouraged and perhaps quit the ministry. So for him, he was battling for Mark's life. Paul, on the other hand, was committed to the success of the mission. He understood that if the desertion happened again, it could derail the ministry and cause much damage among the churches. Paul could not allow that to happen.
- So what did they do? They agreed to disagree and came up with a solution that was good for both parties. Barnabas would take John Mark with him, and Paul would include Silas as his disciple on the journey.
- In the sovereignty of God, out of this disagreement came a doubling of their labor, for Barnabas went to strengthen the churches in Cyprus and Paul went to the churches in Syria, Cilicia, and then Galatia. In addition, both of their disciples (Mark and Silas) went on to have significant ministries themselves. Sometimes sharp disagreement can lead to more fruitfulness!

NOTES

4. Acts 16:1-40

A. There are three paragraphs in *Chapter 16*:
- *16:1-5* – <u>Timothy joins Paul and Silas</u>. Because Timothy's mother was Jewish, Paul had him circumcised before their trip. They continued on the way, revisiting the churches on the first mission.
- *16:6-10* – <u>Paul is called to Macedonia</u>. Through divine direction Paul was led to the town of Troas, where he received a vision directing him to witness in the Greek province of Macedonia.
- *16:11-40* – <u>Paul witnesses in Philippi</u>. Philippi was the first Macedonian city in which Paul witnessed. His ministry there is related in four parts: the conversion of Lydia (*v. 11-14*), the arrest of Paul and Silas (*v. 16-24*), the conversion of the Philippian jailer (*v. 25-34*), and the release of Paul and Silas by the magistrates (*v. 35-40*).

B. Lessons from *Acts 16*
- Follow the leading of the Holy Spirit, even when it doesn't make sense from a human perspective. From Antioch in Pisidia (*v. 6*), Paul and Timothy traveled far northward, and then westward. Natural human wisdom would have led them to think they should preach the Gospel in all the cities that they passed through, but instead the Holy Spirit directed them on a *400-mile (644 km)* journey by foot to Troas (*v. 8*). They must have had a strong sense of the Spirit's direct guidance and concluded that He would give others to preach the Gospel in the Northern regions of Asia and in Bithynia. We read in *1 Peter 1* that Peter had successfully ministered there.
- Be creative in the ministry. Finding no synagogue in Philippi, Paul began his witness in the closet thing to one: a group of women gathered outside the city for prayer (*16:11-15*). One of them, Lydia, responded to the Gospel and was baptized along with her household.
- Learn to be bold in your faith. The jailer's question, *"What must I do to be saved?"* (*16:30*) refers to being saved from the judgment of God, which he would have heard about through listening to his prisoners' prayers and songs.

5. Acts 17:1-34

A. *Chapter 17* contains three paragraphs:
- *17:1-9* – <u>Paul and Silas witness in Thessalonica</u>. From Philippi Paul traveled the *94 miles (151 km)* to Thessalonica, capital of Macedonia. Paul recounts that they had *much boldness in our God to declare to you the Gospel of God in the midst of much conflict*. He also mentions in *Phil 4:16* that the Philippian church helped him with his material needs during this time.
- *17:10-15* – <u>Paul and Silas witness in Berea</u>. Berea is *50 miles (81 km)* by road southwest of Thessalonica.
- *17:16-34* – <u>Paul goes to Athens and witnesses at Mars Hill</u>. Paul's ministry in Athens began in the marketplace, where he encountered some Athenian philosophers (*v. 16-21*). This led to a more formal presentation to the philosophers at their place of meeting, the Areopagus (*v. 22-34*).

B. Lessons from *Acts 17*
- Be known as a great student of the Bible. *Verse 11* tells us that the Bereans were more fair-minded than those in Thessalonica because *they received the Word with all readiness, searching the Scriptures daily to see if these things were so.*
- The Christian faith has credible reasons and ample evidence that point to its truthfulness. Knowing for sure that Jesus had been raised from the dead gave Paul and the other Apostles great confidence in witnessing, even to intellectuals like the ones they encountered in Mars Hill. Knowing the truth and being certain of it gives us great confidence and powerful boldness in witnessing.
- Witnessing for Christ is a matter of patient persuasion. Although Paul saw a few people come to faith here in Athens (*v. 34*), he had no helpers with him, and there is no record of any miracles being done.
- Expect your converts to become future ministry leaders. One of the people who came to Christ in Athens was Dionysius the Areopagite, who church history tells us later became the leader of the entire Christian movement in Athens. Though we don't know how he was discipled, we do know he became a leader of great influence.

6. *Acts 18*

A. *Chapter 18* contains two paragraphs:
- *18:1-17* – Paul goes to Corinth. Corinth was the last major place of witness on Paul's second journey. His original work there (*v. 1-11*) is followed by an account of a specific incident when the Jews brought him to trial before the proconsul (*v. 12-17*). But Paul was able to stay *many days longer* (*v. 18*).
- *18:18-28* – Paul and the team return to Antioch. After completing his Corinthian ministry, Paul returned to Antioch, making a brief stop at Ephesus (*v. 18-22*).

B. Lessons from *Acts 18*
- The New Testament teaches that the Christian minister is always worthy of being paid for his work in the ministry (*1 Timothy 5:18*). However, there are times when we must become creative in making money to support our involvement in the Great Commission. Sometimes Paul supplemented his income by making tents (see *v. 3* and also *1 Corinthians 9*).
- We must be committed to both evangelism *and* discipleship. Paul was not only committed to preaching the Gospel where it had not been previously preached (*Romans 15:20*) but also to strengthen the believers wherever he went (see *Acts 18 22-23*).
- Leaders train other leaders. Apollos had only heard a partial message of Christianity. He *knew only the baptism of John*, which suggests that he had not heard about the death, burial and resurrection of Jesus. The husband-wife ministry team of Aquila and Priscilla took him and explained to him the way of God more accurately. As a result, Apollos began to preach the Gospel effectively, powerfully refuting the Jews in public, showing by the Scriptures that Jesus was the Messiah.

NOTES

7. Acts 19:1-41

A. There are three paragraphs in *Acts 19*
- *19:1-10* – <u>Paul encounters the disciples of John</u>. At Ephesus Paul led some disciples of John the Baptist to Christ. It was obvious that these God-fearers were believers, but they had not heard the complete story of the work of Christ. They had obviously been taught by Apollos (*chapter 18*), who taught them as much truth as he knew before he left for Corinth (*v. 1*). Paul came along and finished the story for them, telling about who Jesus was and why He came to earth. God-fearers must take the next step and come to Jesus Christ.
- *19:11-22* – <u>Paul encounters false religion at Ephesus</u>. Paul worked many miracles in Ephesus (*v. 11-12*), but he encountered others who pursued a false way of working "miracles," including some would-be Jewish exorcists (*v. 13-16*), and persons who had a background of faith in magical spirits (*v. 17-20*).
- *19:23-41* – <u>Paul experiences violent opposition at Ephesus</u>. The account of Paul's ministry at Ephesus concludes with a riot against Paul that was provoked by a silversmith named Demetrius.

B. Lessons from *Acts 19*
- Truth transforms people's lives. The followers of John the Baptist had been taught well by Apollos. Unfortunately, at that point in their life they had not heard about the resurrection of Jesus. When Paul came, he asked them questions to see where they were in their understanding. Questions are a great method of discerning where people are at in their journey of faith. Once you know where they are in their understanding, you will be able to take the Word of God and help them progress in the faith.
- Spiritual battle is real. Satan is alive on earth. He is described as the great deceiver, and the enemy of our souls. Here, Satan uses some of his many evil spirits to hinder the work of God. We must stand firm against him and not fall into his temptations. *James 4:7-10* is a great passage about resisting the enemy and remaining pure inwardly and outwardly before the Lord.

8. Acts 20:1-38

A. There are three paragraphs in *Acts 20*
- *20:1-6* – <u>Paul completes his ministry in Greece</u>. Paul makes a final visit to the churches of Macedonia and Achaia, spending the winter in Greece.
- *20:7-16* – <u>Paul travels to Miletus</u>. The journey to Jerusalem continued, with an incident at Troas in which Paul restored the life of a young man (*v. 7-12*). This is followed by a detailed description of the voyage to Miletus (*v. 13-16*).
- *20:17-38* – <u>Paul addresses the Ephesian elders at Miletus</u>. Paul's sermon here is the only example in *Acts* of a major speech to Christians. All of Paul's other speeches were evangelistic and directed toward non-believers. Of all Paul's speeches, it has the most in common with his letters, which of course were addressed to Christians. Paul used his own ministry as an example for the Ephesian elders (*v. 18-21*), spoke of his future pros-

pects (*v. 22-27*), warned of coming heresies (*v. 28-31*), and encouraged a proper attitude toward material goods (*v. 32-35*). The passage ends with a touching display of emotions as the Ephesians realized they would never see Paul again (*v. 36-38*).

B. Lessons from *Acts 20*
- *Verses 7-12* record a miracle of compassion. It was probably embarrassing to Paul that Eutychus fell asleep during his long sermon. Perhaps it was due to the heat from the evening lamps. Paul rushed downstairs and, in a miracle very similar to one performed by Jesus, brought him back to life. The young boy's name, Eutychus, means *lucky*. God goes way beyond this... nothing is luck in the Kingdom of God.
- We must be bold in evangelism. We should follow the example of Paul, who never backed down from declaring the Gospel (*v. 20*).
- Will we stay committed to Jesus' mission for our entire lives? Paul did. See *verse 24*, where Paul says that he did not value his own life. What he was passionate about was the ministry Jesus had given him.
- Invest in the development of leaders in the church. Paul spent time training the leaders at Ephesus (and all the cities in which he planted churches).
- It is very obvious that Paul cared deeply for these believers, and that they cared deeply for him. It is proper for Christians to feel deeply for each other – and to openly display those emotions.
- I want to help you here with something that is very important. Paul told these church leaders that they were to *pay careful attention* to themselves and their doctrine. In other words, *how they lived* and *what they taught* were two of the most critical elements in a new church. Leaders must model the godly characteristics of the life of Jesus. They must also teach sound doctrine. To fall short in either of these areas is to disqualify yourself for church leadership. You *must* pay close attention to living a life that is completely dedicated to Jesus and to teaching the Word of God correctly.
- The leaders (elders) of the church were to *care for the church of God* (*v. 28*). It is the church that Jesus died for. He obtained our salvation through the shedding of His blood on the cross. If He was willing to do that for us, what must we be willing to do to help our churches?
- Paul told them in *verses 29-30* that after he left Ephesus, he knew that false teachers would come to attack the church and lead them astray from Christ. How do you prepare a church to stand firm against false teaching? By teaching them the Word of God! Make sure your church knows the truth. Make sure they know what the Bible teaches, so when false teachers come around, they will be able to stand firm.
- What Paul is describing here – and what you read about in many other situations in the book of *Acts* – is about spiritual battle. You will have an entire section of one of your courses devoted to spiritual battle later in your training, but it is important to note here that spiritual battle is real. The devil and his demons will not be pleased that you are planting a church. They will attempt to stop your efforts, to discourage you, and perhaps even to bring persecution against you. This is where you must be strong and depend on God alone. He is your strength. Jesus is the Way, the Truth, and the Life (see *John 14:6*). Be confident that you are His messen-

NOTES

ger and that nothing Satan does can ultimately stop the advancement of the church. Pray, trust God, keep on the full armor of God (see *Ephesians 6*) and walk closely with Jesus.

- Again in *verse 33*, Paul says that he coveted no one's silver, gold or clothing. Those of us in the ministry must not be in love with the things of this world. You must not covet money. It is easy to fall into temptation in this area – but you must stand firm and resist the temptation to get rich in the ministry.
- In *verse 32*, Paul commended these men to God's care. In other words, he knew that once he was gone, they would need the spiritual strength and empowerment that only God could provide. There will be times in your ministry that you have done all that you can do... and you must simply leave people – and churches – in the care of God. Know that He will take care of them. He is a faithful Shepherd and will protect them when you are gone.

9. *Acts 21:1-40*

A. There are three paragraphs in *Acts 21*
- *21:1-16* – <u>Paul travels to Jerusalem</u>. He journeyed by sea and by land. Along the way he had sorrowful farewells and ominous warnings from each Christian community about the dangers facing him in Jerusalem. The warnings are similar to the ones that accompanied Jesus on His own journey to Jerusalem (*Luke 13:33-35; 18:31-33*).
- *21:17-26* – <u>Paul participates in a Nazirite ceremony</u>. When Paul arrived in Jerusalem, the Christians rejoiced over the success of his Gentile mission but expressed concern over rumors that he was teaching Jews to abandon their ancestral laws and customs. To disprove the rumors, they asked Paul to participate publicly in a Nazirite vow, as specified in the Old Testament law (*Numbers 6:1-21*).
- *21:27-40* – <u>Paul is attacked by an angry mob</u>, and eventually rescued by the Romans.

B. Lessons from *Acts 21*
- Several of the prophecies given about Paul in Tyre told him *through the Spirit... not to go on to Jerusalem*. But this contradicts the story where it says Paul was being guided by the Holy Spirit to go to Jerusalem (see *19:21; 20:22-24; 21:14*). Interpreters differ over how much of what these disciples told Paul was actually part of their prophesying (or *speaking through the Spirit*).
  ▶ Some hold that this incident shows there are two potentials kinds of problems with early Christian prophecies: first that there could be mistakes in the prophecies themselves, and second that there could be mistakes in the prophet's own interpretation. This then would be an example of why Paul commands that prophecies must be tested, that is, to guard against both possible mistakes. See *1 Cor. 14:29; 1 The. 5:21*.
  ▶ Other interpreters believe that, although such prophecies themselves are completely accurate (because they come *through the Spirit*), there still could be mistakes in the interpretation of the prophecy. Thus,

even though the prophecy is accurate, such prophecies still need to be tested.

10. *Acts 22:1-30*

A. There are two paragraphs in *Acts 22*
  - *Acts 22:1-21* – Paul addresses the Jewish crowd. Paul's address establishes his faithfulness to his Jewish heritage. He gave his personal testimony: his former zeal for Judaism (*22:3-5*), his encounter with the risen Lord (*22:6-11*), his commission (*22:12-16*), and his vision in the temple (*22:17-21*)
  - *22:22-30* – Paul reveals his Roman citizenship. As the riot against Paul continued, the tribune took him into the barracks and stretched him on a torture rack. Paul stopped the proceedings by revealing his Roman citizenship.

B. Lessons from *Acts 22*
  - One of the greatest tools in the ministry is your personal testimony of how you came to faith in Jesus. The best way to write out your testimony is to think of it in three parts:
    ▶ What your life was like before you met Jesus. Do not dwell on your sin. Simply tell your story.
    ▶ How you came to believe in Him as your Savior. Include a clear presentation of the Gospel so those who hear you will know how they can also be saved.
    ▶ How Jesus has changed you and brought you to the place you are now. Be specific and talk about the way your life is different because of Jesus. Make sure that the focus of your testimony is on the grace of God in your life and be sure to give the glory to God alone.
  - God does not waste anything from your past. Paul's status as a Roman citizen protected him.

11. *Acts 23:1-35*

A. There are two paragraphs in *Acts 23*
  - *23:1-22* – Zealous Jews plot against Paul. Unable to get any answers by scourging, the tribune turned to the Jewish court for help. Paul's nephew informed the tribune of a plot by 40 zealous Jews to kill him.
  - *23:23-35* – Paul is delivered to Governor Felix. To protect Paul, the tribune sent him at night and by heavy guard to the governor in Caesarea.

B. Lessons from *Acts 23*
  - God is glorified through our trials. And many times, doors for effective ministry will open during those times. In these chapters, Paul is given many opportunities to share Christ:
    ▶ With religious leaders (*23:1-11*).
    ▶ With political leaders (*24:1-21; 25:23-26:23*).
    ▶ With sailors (*27:13-26*).
    ▶ With islanders (*28:1-10*).

NOTES

- What opportunities is God giving you to tell others about Jesus?[33]
- Sometimes relatives are seen at just the right moment to assist in God's agenda.

12. *Acts 24:1-27*

A. There is one paragraph in *Acts 24*
- *Acts 24:1-27* – <u>Paul appears before Felix</u>. The closest thing to an actual trial for Paul took place before Felix when the Jewish group arrived from Jerusalem bringing their charges against him. Felix was not persuaded, and he dismissed the court, but continued to hold Paul in custody, frequently conversing with him privately.

B. Lessons from *Acts 24*
- We must learn to trust God in all of our circumstances. Sometimes what seems to us to be a closed door is really God at work accomplishing His purposes. Imprisoned in Caesarea for more than two years, Paul received formal hearings from the governors Felix, Festus and the Jewish king Agrippa II. When Festus decided to take him to Jerusalem for trial, Paul appealed for trial in Rome before the emperor. Going to Rome was Paul's ultimate goal... and God took him there, all at the expense of the Roman government.
- Use wisdom and timing in your appeals.

13. *Acts 25:1-27*

A. There are two paragraphs in *Acts 25*
- *Acts 25:1-12* – <u>Paul appeals to Caesar</u>. The new procurator Festus wanted to win the favor of his people. When approached by the Jewish leaders concerning Paul, he at first resisted but later gave in to their desire to try Paul in Jerusalem. To avoid the fate that awaited him there, Paul invoked his citizen's right of appeal for trial before the emperor.
- *Acts 25:13-27* – <u>Paul is allowed to present his case to King Agrippa II</u>.

B. Lessons from *Acts 25*
- Humility ought to be the mark of each believer. But humility does not mean that we are never to stand up for our rights. Paul appealed for his right of trial before the Roman emperor.
- The Bible is truthful in all it records. Luke, the author of the book of *Acts*, goes into great historical detail to tell us the facts behind Paul's trials.

14. *Acts 26:1-32*

A. There is one paragraph in *Acts 26*
- *Acts 26:1-32* – <u>Paul witnesses to King Agrippa</u>. Paul testifies before the king (in fulfillment of Jesus' prophesy in *9:15*). Of the three speeches where Paul defended himself (*chapters 22, 24, 26*), this one before Agrippa gives the most detailed exposition of the Gospel.

B. Lessons from *Acts 26*
- Jesus opens doors that no man can shut – and He shuts doors that no man can open (*Rev 3:8*). When God opens a door to proclaim the Gospel, we must be ready. How do you prepare yourself to be ready? Pray, study, and look for the open doors that God provides.

15. *Acts 27:1-44*

A. There is one paragraph in *Acts 27*
- *Acts 27:1-44* – Paul travels to Rome by sea. The last two chapters of *Acts* are devoted mainly to Paul's journey to Rome. In Rome, he followed his usual pattern of beginning with the Jews then turning to all who would come and listen to his message.

B. Lessons from *Acts 27*
- God is sovereign over all of life. He protected Paul – and He will protect you. The voyage to Rome, (which probably began in the fall of *AD 59*), is given in great detail and with remarkable exactness, consistent with what is otherwise known about sea travel in that time and place. The keynote of the story is God's providence, especially in preserving Paul for his Roman testimony. The story is told to indicate how far and difficult the journey to Rome is. Here, the Gospel continues to reach the ends of the earth.

16. *Acts 28:1-31*

A. There are three paragraphs in *Acts 28*
- *Acts 28:1-10* – Paul witnesses on the island of Malta. The shipwrecked travelers spent the remainder of the winter on the island of Malta. Paul's time there is highlighted by his protection from a snake bite (*v. 1-6*) and his healing of the leading citizen's father (*v. 7-10*).
- *Acts 28:11-16* – Paul finally arrives in Rome. The fact that Paul was able to live in his own housing points to his high status as a prisoner and perhaps to the support of local believers.
- *Acts 28:17-31* – Paul witnesses to the Jews in Rome. He has arrived at his goal, and though he is unable to visit the synagogues himself, he invited the Roman Jews to come to him.

B. Lessons from *Acts 28*
- Paul shared the Gospel with all who came to him, including both Jews and Gentiles. This situation continued for two years (*AD 60-62*), at which time Luke's account ends.
- Information as to what happened next comes from extra-biblical sources and from hints in the last few of Paul's letters. One church historian says that Paul preached *in the limits of the west*, which may indicate the fulfillment of his desire to preach in Spain (see *Romans 15:24*).[34] This would also point to his release from his first Roman imprisonment. A church historian, writing in *AD 325*,[35] cites the tradition that Paul was freed from confinement and carried on a further ministry until he was arrested and placed in a second Roman imprisonment, at which time he was martyred.

- In God's sovereignty, Paul's time was not wasted, for it was during his Roman imprisonment that he wrote the letters to the Ephesians, Philippians, Colossians, and Philemon. The time after Paul's release from his first imprisonment (mid-60's) would be when he wrote *1 Timothy* and *Titus*. He probably wrote his last letter, *2 Timothy*, during his second imprisonment, as he awaited execution (*2 Tim 4:6-8*).
- I just saw something in my study of *Acts* that I have not seen in almost forty years of walking with Jesus. (Isn't it wonderful that we keep learning new things? The Word of God is limitless in its wisdom and insight!) What I saw was the very last words of the book of *Acts*. *Verse 31* tells us that Paul was *preaching the Kingdom of God and teaching the things which concern the Lord Jesus Christ with all confidence, no one forbidding him*. The very last words of the book of *Acts* tell us that the Gospel was *unhindered*. God had provided that open door for Paul to preach the Gospel. Unhindered. That is my prayer for you. Plant your church…and pray that God will open a door so wide that the Gospel will be unhindered, and that your ministry will grow and expand, and that for years to come, people in your village, region and throughout your country will hear the Gospel because it is *unhindered*.

Chapter 11
Paul: The World's Greatest Church Planter

Introduction

While they were worshiping the Lord and fasting, the Holy Spirit said, "Set apart for me Barnabas and Saul (later known as Paul) for the work to which I have called them." Then after fasting and praying they laid their hands on them and sent them off (Acts 13:2-3).

History records that the world's greatest theologian was also the greatest church planter.[36] His ministry is the principle focus of the second half of the book of Acts. *Acts 13-28* is ordered around the three missionary journeys that Paul led throughout Asia Minor.

1. A Brief Survey of Paul's Life

A. Paul was born "Saul," a Roman citizen in a Greek city, Tarsus. Yet he was born in a Jewish family and was educated in a Hebrew school in Jerusalem.

B. His education was superior. He studied under one of the leading teachers of the day, Gamaliel. After Gamaliel died, it was said of him: *The glory of the Torah ceased, and purity and saintliness perished.*

C. Though fiercely anti-Christian, Paul was converted to "The Way" after he had an encounter with the risen Christ on his way to arrest Christians in Damascus. "The Way" was how early Christians referred to Jesus, who had said He was *the Way, the Truth and the Life* (see *John 14:6*).

D. His early years as a Christian are unclear. Thirteen years after his conversion, he took up a ministry position in Antioch, at the invitation of Barnabas.

E. Though born and educated as a Jew, Paul had special concern for non-Jews. That's why Barnabas invited him to Antioch, why Paul defended the authenticity of Gentile Christians' faith before Peter and other Jerusalem church leaders, and why he set out on a special missionary journey to Greek cities in Asia Minor (Turkey).

F. In every Greek city he visited, Paul first preached to the Jews. He would attend a synagogue service, and when the invitation was given to visitors to address the congregation (a common custom), he would talk about Jesus as Messiah.

G. Paul made his way into Europe on his second missionary journey, planting churches in many cities in Greece. Sometimes he evangelized one-on-one, as he did with Lydia in Philippi (*Acts 16*); other times he preached to synagogue audiences (*Acts 17:2-3*); other times, to the Greek philosophers (*Acts 17:16-34*).

H. Paul never worked alone. On his missionary journeys, he was accompanied by Barnabas, Silas, Timothy, Titus, and Luke among others.

I. Though Paul was determined to spread the Gospel far and wide, he settled down twice in his ministry for extensive stays in Corinth (18 months) and Ephesus (nearly three years). Both were multi-ethnic cities, and leading centers of pagan religions. Both cities had huge tourism industries.

J. Paul didn't let anything get in the way of spreading the message. Even when he was under arrest, he proclaimed his Gospel to each authority he stood before, and when under house arrest in Rome, he invited people into his place to preach to them.

K. In addition to his extensive travels in Palestine, Asia Minor, and Greece, some historians believe Paul also visited regions today known as Spain and Yugoslavia.

L. Though Paul wasn't a good public speaker by the standards of the day (*1 Cor. 2:1 – 4*), he nonetheless preached regularly.

M. In sheer numbers, many modern evangelists have reached more people for Christ than did Paul. But none have had his enduring impact: the founding of churches in a variety of cultures, which spawned more churches in other cultures, so that the church continued to grow until it dominated all of European society.

2. What Shaped Paul into a Great Leader?

It is natural to look at a leader like Paul and to conclude that the reason for his success and impact was that he was highly gifted. And certainly Paul was. But I believe there were some other reasons – reasons that we don't normally see. Yet, if we become aware of them, we can reproduce and replicate them today.

A. Paul was Discipled and Encouraged by Barnabas

Barnabas was one of the leaders of the early Church movement. His name meant *Son of Encouragement*. Everywhere he went he encouraged believers. His relationship with Paul was no different. He knew that Paul, like everyone, needed someone who believed in him.

In Acts 9:27, Barnabas took hold of Paul and brought him to the Apostles to prove that he had legitimately become a Christian. When the church at Antioch was growing and needing more leaders, Barnabas went to Tarsus to look for Saul. He found him and brought him to Antioch and for an entire year Barnabas and Paul met with the church there and taught considerable numbers of believers (*Acts 11:25-26*).

Yes, Barnabas did see the potential for great things in Paul's life. But I believe Barnabas saw that in *everyone's* life that he knew.

> **Assignment:**
>
> How can you encourage the new believers that are in your church plant in the same way Barnabas encouraged Paul?

B. Paul Came Out of a Great Church Ministry

The Church at Antioch was one of the healthiest churches in the New Testament. And though Paul, as a leader, was responsible for shaping that healthy church, it is also true that the church was responsible for shaping Paul.

As we plant churches, it is most important to insure their health. The church at Antioch was one example of a very healthy church.

> **Assignment:**
>
> Read the story about the first century church found in Antioch (*Acts 11:19-30; 13:1-3; 14:26-38; 15:1-33 and 18:22-23*). Note the following *14 observations* about a healthy church.
>
> - They experienced God's approval and His power was with them. *Acts 11:21 – And the hand of the Lord was with them...*
> - They experienced great conversion growth. *Acts 11:21 - And a great number believed and turned to the Lord.*
> - They embraced help from others. *Acts 11:22-24 – Then news of these things came to the ears of the church in Jerusalem, and they sent out Barnabas to go as far as Antioch. When he came and had seen the grace of God, he was glad, and encouraged them all that with purpose of heart they should continue with the Lord. For he was a good man, full of the Holy Spirit and of faith. And a great many people were added to the Lord.*
> - They were a place where leaders were developed. *Acts 11:25-26 - Then Barnabas departed for Tarsus to seek Saul. And when he had found him, he brought him to Antioch. So it was that for a whole year they assembled with the church and taught a great many people. And the disciples were first called Christians in Antioch.*
> - They deeply and broadly penetrated their culture. *Acts 11:26 - The disciples were first called Christians in Antioch.*
> - They were people of great generosity. *Acts 11:27-30 – And in these days prophets came from Jerusalem to Antioch. Then one of them, named Agabus, stood up and showed by the Spirit that there was going to be a great famine throughout all the world, which also happened in the days of Claudius Caesar. Then the disciples, each according to his ability, determined to send relief to the brethren dwelling in Judea.*

> *This they also did, and sent it to the elders by the hands of Barnabas and Saul.*
> - They were a church led by cross-cultural, multi-ethnic leaders. *Acts 13:1 – Now in the church at Antioch there were certain prophets and teachers: Barnabas, Simeon who was called Niger, Lucius of Cyrene, Manaen who had been brought up with Herod the tetrarch and Saul.*
> - They were a church that had leaders who prioritized ministering to the Lord, fasting and prayer. *Acts 13:2 – As they ministered to the Lord and fasted.*
> - They were a church whose leaders listened to the Holy Spirit and obeyed His call. *Acts 13:2 ...the Holy Spirit said, 'Now separate to me Barnabas and Saul for the work to which I have called them.'*
> - They were a church who willingly released their top leaders for God's appointed ministry. *Acts 13:3 – Then, having fasted and prayed and laid hands on them, they sent them away.*
> - They were a home base for cross-cultural church planters. *Acts 14:26-28 – From there they sailed to Antioch, where they had been commended to the grace of God for the work which they had completed. Now when they had come and gathered the church together, they reported all that God had done with them, and that He had opened the door of faith to the Gentiles. So they stayed there a long time with the disciples.*
> - They created an environment where theology was developed and corrected. *Acts 15:1-2 – And certain men came down from Judea and taught the brethren, "Unless you are circumcised according to the custom of Moses, you cannot be saved. Therefore, when Paul and Barnabas had no small dissension and dispute with them, they determined that Paul and Barnabas and certain others of them should go up to Jerusalem, to the apostles and elders, about this question.*
> - They were key players in seeing a movement of churches started. *Acts 18:22-23 – And when he had landed at Caesarea, and gone up and greeted the church, he went down to Antioch. After he had spent some time there, he departed and went over the region of Galatia and Phrygia in order, strengthening all the disciples.*

C. Paul Combined Good Theology with Passionate and Effective Ministry

Paul wrote some of the greatest doctrinal books ever (*Romans, Galatians, Ephesians*, etc.). He was known for his superior intellect and his great grasp of deep doctrinal truths. In *2 Corinthians 12:1-6*, Paul describes how he was caught up into Paradise and taught great visions and revelations from God. But he was also passionate about expanding the Church to the ends of the earth. He was a great church planter. At the end of his life he could faithfully declare that he had fought the good fight, finished the course God had for him, and kept the faith (*2 Timothy 4:6-8*). He was faithful... and fruitful.

D. Paul had a great heart for evangelism.
- To spread the message, he made great sacrifices (including the hardships of travel, persecution, and being put in jail).
- He took full advantage of his background (as both Jew and Roman citizen) to reach diverse groups.
- He tailored the message to the culture of each audience.
- He changed his strategy depending on the circumstances (staying in some cities only shortly, others for years at a time).
- He took advantage of each circumstance to present the message (when free or in prison; whether in front of a crowd or a single individual).
- He did what needed doing, whether he was particularly gifted or not (e.g., his limited preaching skills). He was as gifted as anyone as a teacher. He knew his gifts.
- He worked in a team (with Barnabas, Silas, Luke, Timothy, Titus, etc.).
- Within limits, he let people give free expression to the working of the Spirit.

Assignment:

Read *2 Timothy 4:1-5*. What do you learn about Paul? What did he stress to his young disciple Timothy?

Chapter 12
Biblical Theology of Evangelism

Introduction

> *When the people heard this, they were cut to the heart and said to Peter and the other apostles, "Brothers, what shall we do?" Peter replied, "Repent and be baptized, every one of you, in the name of Jesus Christ for the forgiveness of your sins. And you will receive the gift of the Holy Spirit. The promise is for you and your children and for all who are far off—for all whom the Lord our God will call." With many other words he warned them; and he pleaded with them, "Save yourselves from this corrupt generation." Those who accepted his message were baptized, and about three thousand were added to their number that day (Acts 2:37-41).*

What is evangelism? What is the purpose of evangelism? Often it is either misunderstood or separated into one of the 'ministries' that churches "do." Some people say they have the gift of evangelism or that they are called to be an 'evangelist.' What does that mean? Are they somehow more qualified than others to reach unbelievers with the Gospel?

Let's start with a definition ...

> **Assignment:**
>
> Before reading ahead, how would you define evangelism?

1. The Definition of Evangelism

A. Simply, evangelism is telling others about Jesus and what He has done for them. Bill Bright, founder and former president of Campus Crusade for Christ, said: *Evangelism is simply telling others about Christ in the power of the Holy Spirit and leaving the results to God*. I like that definition because it contains three essential elements:
- Content – telling others about Christ. Evangelism isn't just telling others about your church or inviting them to come to church, though that it a good thing. Evangelism has content: telling others of the death and resurrection of Jesus and how we can be reconciled to Him.
- Empowerment – witnessing is never to be done *in the flesh*. We must be filled with the Spirit (*Ephesians 5:18*) in order to be effective communicators of the Gospel.
- Results – we must leave the results to God. It is God's responsibility to save people. We must leave that in His hands.

B. We must present good theology as we share the Gospel.
   - The Bible speaks of *another* Gospel – a different and distorted Gospel that adds legalism and the law to grace, repentance and faith in Christ (*Gal. 1:6-9*).
   - Appeals based on materialism and only the benefits *in this life* should be avoided (*1 Tim. 6:6*).
   - There are *false Gospels, false Christ's, false apostles, and false teachings* that will continue to permeate the church until the return of Christ (*2 Tim. 4:3-4*).
   - Our command is to preach the Word (*2 Tim 4:2*).

C. The foundational facts of the Gospel are that Jesus Christ was crucified, buried, and raised from the dead (*1 Corinthians 15:1-4*).

D. The Gospel includes both *repentance and faith*.
   - Sinners must believe in Jesus Christ, repenting of their sin (*Mark 1:15, 6:12, Acts 17:30*).
   - Sinners believe by having faith in Jesus Christ for their salvation (*Rom. 10:9-10*).
   - Faith comes by hearing, and hearing by the Word (*Rom 10:17*).

2. Effective Evangelism Begins with Prayer[37]

A. Prayer is *essential* for reaching the lost.
   - Prayer communicates our dependence upon God.
   - We should pray first that God would open a door for the Word to be preached – *Colossians 4:2-6*.
   - We should pray that God would open the hearts and minds of unbelievers so they would see God's glory and the truth of the Gospel.
   - *Never let them perish for lack of your supplications.*[38]

B. Prayer properly emphasizes God's power and work in evangelism.

C. Pray for someone who doesn't know the Lord each day.

3. Evangelism is More than an 'Event'

A. Jesus at times spoke to large crowds but more frequently to individuals (Nicodemus in *John 3*; Samaritan woman at the well in *John 4*; etc).

B. Evangelism can sometimes result in an immediate conversion to Christ. However, there are times when a person must hear repeated presentations of the Gospel before they come to faith. This is due in part to the fact that there are some people close to coming to Christ and others who are very far away from Him. In addition, sometimes it takes time for the Holy Spirit's work to break through. The Holy Spirit desires to pull the spiritual blinders off of those without Christ.

4. There Are Many Different Evangelism Strategies that Are Effective

A. One-on-one presentations of the Gospel. This can occur with friends, family, fellow workers, and anyone/everyone we meet during our day.

B. Large evangelistic meetings.

C. Inviting people to church to be part of a worship service where they hear a presentation of the Gospel.

D. A special event, such as a showing of *The Jesus Film*[39] or some other evangelistic strategy.

E. Small groups where non-believers are welcomed and taught about the Christian faith.

F. Attraction strategies. This is a method that invites people to visit or reach an audience that normally otherwise would not consider the claims of Christ. Christians invite nonbelievers to their homes, to their church meetings, or to some event where there will be Christian fellowship. It is positive in that it proclaims Jesus' invitation to "come to Me" (*John 7:37*).

G. Befriending non-Christians and getting to know them personally, ultimately looking for an opportunity to talk with them about Jesus. Evangelism wasn't meant to be a presentation only, but a lifestyle lived out daily in normal cultural contacts.[40]

H. A healthy balance in evangelism should include intercession, inspiration, invitation, conversion, AND discipleship. Evangelism is more about a lifestyle for all God's people than just a ministry program for some of God's people, and…the Gospel is made clearest by the honest words and open lives of those who have been transformed by grace.[41] There are many appropriate strategies for reaching people with the Gospel. You must understand what will work in your culture and in your church.

I. One misconception that many people have is that witnessing is simply living a good life in front of other people. There are two problems with this view:
- It misrepresents the faith. Christianity isn't *being nice, kind and doing good things*. Christianity is knowing that we are sinners, separated from God, deserving of eternal hell, and that we have been rescued, delivered and redeemed by Jesus. *Living a good life* and hoping people figure out Christianity because of our good deeds sends the wrong message.
- This strategy isn't very effective. It places its hope on the popular statement; *Preach Christ at all times, and if necessary, use words.*[42] The idea is that we preach the Gospel not with words, but with deeds. It is true that we are to live in such a way that unbelievers will ask us the reason for the hope we have (*1 Peter 3:15*). However, apart from hearing the Gospel, no one will ever come to faith. *Romans 10:14-15* states, *How then will they call on Him in whom they have not believed? How will they believe in Him*

whom they have not heard? And how will they hear without a preacher? How will they preach unless they are sent?

5. Every Christian is Called to Do the Work of an Evangelist

But you, be sober in all things, endure hardship, do the work of an evangelist, fulfill your ministry (2 Tim 4:5).

A. There is a role of 'Evangelist' described in Scripture: *Acts 21:8, Eph 4:11*.

B. The primary purpose of the Evangelist role is not only to present the Gospel to people (sometimes in large group situations, sometimes one-on-one) but also to equip other believers to learn to clearly, accurately and relevantly communicate their faith (*Eph 4:12*).

C. There is not a specific *gift of evangelism* listed in the spiritual gift lists in Scripture. However, all believers are called to tell others about Jesus.

D. Pastors are called to do the work of an evangelist, both teaching the saints how to evangelize, as well as presenting the Gospel publically.

6. The Content of the Gospel is Known as the Good News

A. The word *Gospel* means good news. It is the good news of who Jesus is and what He accomplished by His life, death and resurrection (*1 Cor. 15:1-4*).

B. The Gospel is good news especially in the context of the *bad* news that we are sinners, separated from God by our sin, born spiritually dead and deserving of eternal hell (*Rom. 3:10; 3:23; 5:12; 6:23; Gen. 3*).

C. The Gospel tells us that we can be redeemed (bought out of the slave market of sin by the blood of Christ), forgiven, justified (declared righteous in God's sight) and made into new creatures loved by God (*Rom. 5:8; 5:19; 8:1-4; 2 Cor. 5:17*).
   - The means of obtaining salvation is through repentance from sin and faith toward God – not legalistic righteousness (*Eph. 2:8-9, Phi. 3:9*).
   - The triumph of Jesus over sin, death, the unrighteous, and all kingdoms of the earth brings eternal glory to God (*Psa. 2; Rom. 8:24; Phi. 2:9-11; Eph. 1:21*).

D. Though good works do not save us, good works are the logical and necessary result of being saved by grace through faith (*Eph. 2:8-10*).
   - A lifestyle can communicate the Gospel to the unbelieving world (*Heb 13:15-16*). We are called to be salt and light (*Mat. 5:13-16*) and to be living letters to the world (*2 Cor. 3:2-3*).
   - How many times have we seen Christians engage in one-shot evangelism where the Gospel is presented and then move on to the next person when a favorable spiritual decision does not happen? We will never see our world transformed using these all-too-common evangelism techniques. We need to engage in life-on-life relationships if transformation is ever to take place.[43]

- There is a direct relationship between the power of the Gospel being lived out in the lives of people in a community and how much that community is altered by the Gospel.[44]

7. Evangelism is Necessary for Fulfilling the Great Commission

A. All Christians are called to be *ambassadors*, representing God to the world and proclaiming the Gospel everywhere (*2 Corinthians 5:18-21; 5:17-21*).
   - An ambassador *represents someone other than himself* at the court of someone else.
   - An ambassador does *not live for himself*, but for the one he represents.
   - An ambassador is a spokesman for the person they represent, and are expected to live and make decisions as if the person themselves were present.

B. The entire church should be mobilized, not simply one or two people sent out occasionally. Pastors must constantly and consistently encourage and equip the congregation to be missionaries.

C. Evangelism will continue until the second coming of Christ. (*Mat. 24:14, Mar. 13:10*)

Conclusion

All believers are called to fulfill the Great Commission by sharing their faith and lives with unbelievers. We have been given the ministry of reconciliation and the privilege of seeing men and women become reconciled to their Creator through the proclamation of the Gospel.

Assignment:

As I said earlier, there are many appropriate strategies for reaching people with the Gospel. You must understand what will work in your culture and in your church. What type of strategies will you use to reach people for Jesus?

Chapter 13
How You Can Help Fulfill the Great Commission

Introduction

Now that you are a Christian, you have the great gift of salvation from Jesus Christ. Because you were presented with the Gospel and believed, you have been freed from sin and death and have been given an abundant, eternal life. But millions of people in the world today have not heard the good news about Jesus Christ and so do not have the chance to believe and experience an abundant, eternal life.

In the same way that God desired you to hear the Gospel so that you might believe in His Son Jesus and be saved, He also *desires all men to be saved and to come to the knowledge of the truth* (*1 Timothy 2:4*). This is why Jesus gave us the command to *go into all the world and preach the Gospel to every creature* (*Mark 16:15*) and to *make disciples of all the nations* (*Matthew 28:19*). Bringing the good news of Jesus to the world is called the Great Commission, and this privilege has been given to us as Christians. You can help fulfill the Great Commission by telling those you know about Jesus, by praying for those who do not yet know Him, or by giving your time or money to help allow the Gospel to be preached throughout the world. Ask God about the specific way you can help fulfill the Great Commission.[45]

1. Who Should Be Involved in Fulfilling the Great Commission?

It is not simply pastors and church leaders who should be committed to the fulfillment of the Great Commission. All Christians are called to share their faith and pray for the fulfillment of the Great Commission.

> *Go therefore and make disciples of all the nations, baptizing them in the name of the Father and of the Son and of the Holy Spirit* (*Matthew 28:19*).
>
> *Now then, we are ambassadors for Christ, as though God were pleading through us: we implore you on Christ's behalf, be reconciled to God* (*2 Corinthians 5:20*).
>
> *How beautiful are the feet of those who preach the Gospel of peace, who bring glad tidings of good things!* (*Romans 10:15*).

2. How Can We Reach the World with the Gospel?

   A. Follow God's strategy. *In Acts 1:8*, Jesus told the disciples to begin where they were (Jerusalem) and then allow the Spirit of God to expand their influence to the surrounding villages, cities and countries (Judea and Samaria), and ultimately to the end of the earth.
   - They were first to be witnesses in Jerusalem, their local city. They were to begin with those nearest to them. It should be natural for us to preach the Gospel to our friends, family and those close to us in our lives.

- Then they were to move into Judea, their surrounding countryside. Stepping beyond who we are close with, we should also preach the Gospel and share our faith with people we do not know.
- Next they were to move into Samaria. The Jews hated the Samaritans. They were their political, social and religious enemies. But Jesus told the disciples to love their enemies. There are people we may not prefer to minister to, but we must overcome our biases, prejudices and share Christ's love with them. We are called to reach all people and be a cross cultural church planting ministry.
- This ultimately progresses to the ends of the earth.

B. Be involved in spiritual multiplication. *2 Timothy 2:2* is the key verse for The Timothy Initiative. In that verse, Paul tells his young disciple, Timothy, to invest his life in leaders who will reach others who will reach others. It is not enough to add one believer at a time. Paul tells Timothy to *multiply* his life into men who will *multiply* their lives into others who will *multiply* their lives into others.

C. Rely on the power of the Holy Spirit. *Acts 1:8* tells us that the disciples would receive power when the Holy Spirit came upon them and the natural result of this is that they would be empowered to be His witnesses. The Holy Spirit's presence fell upon the disciples at Pentecost (*Acts 2*) and the rest of the book of *Acts* describes the evangelistic efforts of these empowered disciples. *Acts 4:13* describes the reaction of the enemies of the Gospel: *Now when they saw the boldness of Peter and John, and perceived that they were uneducated and untrained men, they marveled. And they realized that they had been with Jesus.*

D. Make regular prayer for non-believers a part of your church's ministry.

Assignment:

Read *1 Timothy 2:1-7*. What does this passage tell you about praying for those who don't know Christ as their Savior?

E. Church Planting. It should be no surprise by now that the best way to reach people for Jesus is the planting of new churches. In *Titus 1:5* Paul says to his young disciple Titus, *For this reason I left you in Crete, that you should set in order the things that are lacking and appoint elders in every city as I commanded you.* Crete was an island in the Mediterranean Sea. Paul had sent Titus there to plant churches, build leaders and establish growing ministries throughout that island.

When churches do the things God commanded, there will be evangelistic fruit. *Acts 2:46-47* says, *They broke bread in their homes and ate together with glad and sincere hearts, praising God and enjoying the favor of all the people. And the Lord added to their number daily those who were being saved.*

3. What Are the Barriers to Sharing the Gospel?

A. People who don't know Jesus cannot proclaim the Good News if they have not experienced it firsthand. Many claim to know and have a relationship with Jesus, but do not. *Matthew 7:21-2 - Not everyone who says to Me, 'Lord, Lord,' will enter the kingdom of heaven, but he who does the will of My Father who is in heaven will enter. Many will say to Me on that day, 'Lord, Lord, did we not prophesy in Your name, and in Your name cast out demons, and in Your name perform many miracles?' And then I will declare to them, 'I never knew you'.*

B. Fear stops many believers. We must realize the truth that we have not been given a spirit of fear. *2 Timothy 1:7 - For God has not given us a spirit of timidity, but of power and love and discipline.* We should preach Christ with boldness and reverence. *1 Peter 3:15 - But sanctify Christ as Lord in your hearts, always being ready to make a defense to everyone who asks you to give an account for the hope that is in you, yet with gentleness and reverence.*

C. Broken Relationships hinder the advancement of the Gospel. If a relationship is not reconciled and restored, it can be difficult to preach good news to that individual. Before we worship God and serve Him, we must go and be reconciled with those we have offenses with. *Matthew 5:23-24 - Therefore if you are presenting your offering at the altar, and there remember that your brother has something against you, leave your offering there before the altar and go; first be reconciled to your brother, and then come and present your offering.*

4. The Most Critical Element to Fulfilling the Great Commission is Developing Leaders

Leaders are God's method. The theme of the book of *Acts* is the expansion of the Good News of Jesus Christ all over the then known world through Spirit-filled leaders. The main strategy God uses in the planting of new churches is the planting of Spirit filled leaders. This strategy worked then and it still works today.

God's main strategy in church planting is the development and strategic placement of leaders: leaders who are filled and empowered with the Holy Spirit; and leaders who love and teach God's Word. His book is entitled, *The Acts of the Apostles*. It is the *Acts* of the Holy Spirit in the lives of leaders that produces the *Acts* of the Holy Spirit in churches.

E.M. Bounds understood this when he wrote,

> *We are constantly on a stretch to devise new methods, new plans, and new organizations to advance the Church and secure enlargement and efficiency for the Gospel. This trend of the day has a tendency to lose sight of the person or sink the person in the plan or organization. God's plan is to make much of the man or woman, far more of him than of anything else. Men and women are God's method.*

NOTES

> *What the Church needs today is not more machinery or better, not even organizations or more novel methods, but men and women whom the Holy Spirit can use... The Holy Spirit does not flow through methods but through people. He does not come on machinery, but men and women.*[46]

The Church of the *21st century* is fixated on methods and strategies. We can often manipulate and push people through our strategic plans and lose track of the working of the Holy Spirit. This is dangerous.

I hear and read much about strategic plans and creative methods for planting churches. But I hear little about the person who is the leader of the church plant. Yet it is the leader that matters most. It is the leader who is filled with the Spirit that God powerfully uses.

I once asked a leader who had founded a very successful church planting movement, what was the key to effective church planting, and he said, *Being the right person, at the right place, at the right time*. That is so simple, yet very profound. God's Word gives us the best guide for *being the right leader, at the right place, at the right time*.

Assignment:

What are you giving your life to? Is it the Great Commission? How are you building leaders who are committed to the Great Commission?

Chapter 14
Prayer and Evangelism

Introduction

Colossians 4:2-6 – Devote yourselves to prayer, keeping alert in it with an attitude of thanksgiving; praying at the same time for us as well, that God will open up to us a door for the word, so that we may speak forth the mystery of Christ, for which I have also been imprisoned; that I may make it clear in the way I ought to speak. Conduct yourselves with wisdom toward outsiders, making the most of the opportunity. Let your speech always be with grace, as though seasoned with salt, so that you will know how you should respond to each person.

This passage is full of significant insights for the church planter, and it begins with a call to prayer for the purposes of effective evangelism. In this letter penned from a Roman prison, Paul takes time out to instruct the Colossian Christians about the proper strategy and mindset in the proclamation of the Gospel. In fact, I think Paul is giving them – and us – a strategy for telling others the truth. It is a strategy that has ten steps.

1. Focused Prayer – The Responsibility of the Church

First, Paul says that we must devote ourselves to prayer. The word *devote* comes from a word that means *to be strong*. It is used ten times throughout the New Testament, and it always describes a commitment and a strong adherence to a task (See *Acts 1:14; 2:46*). It implies persistence and fervor.

Effectively preaching the Gospel begins with an attitude of dependence, knowing that with all of our persuasiveness and experience, fruitful ministry still ultimately depends upon God. Paul is telling us there that the first step toward effective evangelism is prayer. And he asks for prayer for himself and Timothy as they seek to proclaim the Gospel. Paul understood that one of God's unbreakable laws is to *talk to God about men before talking to men about God*. So he challenges his readers to begin with prayer.

2. An Open Door – God's Response to Our Prayers

The second element is "an open door" (*verse 3*). This is the divine element in evangelism. God must be at work giving an opportunity or an open door for us to proclaim the Gospel. What is an open door? It is an opportunity that allows entrance for the Gospel. It may be a situational opportunity, such as an invitation to preach to a select group of people, or simply realizing that the person sitting next to you as you travel has a background that you can relate to. It may be a group of believers trained in evangelism who are in a particular situation in their jobs that gives them the opportunity to share the Gospel with others. It may even be a loosening of governmental controls on missionary efforts in closed countries. When Paul wrote this epistle he was imprisoned in Rome – but he knew God could open a door, even in prison, for the proclamation of the Gospel.

I believe this open door extends beyond situational opportunities. In *John 6:44* Jesus said, *No one can come to Me, unless the Father who sent Me draws him, and I will raise him up on the last day.* Jesus is speaking about God's work in drawing men and women to come to Christ. Unless God opens the door, drawing people to Himself, we will be ineffective in evangelism.

Unlike the situational open door, where the open door may be quite clearly seen, this open door may not be seen until after the fact. An individual's true identity can only be seen outwardly after he comes to saving faith in Christ. *1 Thessalonians 1:4-5* states, *Knowing, brethren beloved by God, His choice of you; for our Gospel did not come to you in word only, but also in power and in the Holy Spirit and with full conviction.*

In talking with someone, we might be able to see hints of God's drawing process at work. But in large group situations it is a little different. Nevertheless, Paul understood the necessity of this open door quite well. I believe he was asking believers at Colossae to get personally involved in his prison evangelism at Rome by praying for God to open a door to people's hearts drawing them to Christ.

3. Speaking the Word – Our Part as God Opens the Door

The third element in the *Colossians 4* passage is *speaking forth the word*. If the open door is the divine element in the communication process, this is the human element. It's our part. Once God has opened the door, we must take advantage of it and be ready to proclaim the Gospel.

1 Peter 3:15 says we must *sanctify Christ as Lord in your hearts, always being ready to make a defense to everyone who asks you to give an account for the hope that is in you, yet with gentleness and reverence.*

Curtis Vaughan comments, *There was no selfish motive behind (Paul's) prayer; his consuming interest was for the advancement of the Gospel, not for his own blessing.*[47]

Paul writes in *Romans 10:14-15*, *How then will they call on Him in whom they have not believed? How will they believe in Him whom they have not heard? And how will they hear without a preacher? How will they preach unless they are sent? Just as it is written, "How beautiful are the feet of those who bring good news of good things!"*

4. Clarity in Communication – One of Our Prayer Requests

The fourth element that Paul mentions is clearness in communication. In *verse 4*, Paul asks for prayer *in order that I may make it clear in the way I ought to speak.* What a refreshing request! Today most request prayer so they'll survive. Notice the emphasis *is not on Paul.* It's not about him. It's about the Gospel and people hearing and understanding the message. Paul wasn't self-centered in his evangelism. He was others-centered.

We must not simply *quote* Bible verses to people. We must *explain* them. That is exactly what Philip did on the desert road to Gaza (*Acts 8:26-40*). He had a divine appointment (an open door) with a Eunuch (a political leader) from Ethiopia who happened to be reading from the prophet Isaiah's writing in *chapter 53*. Philip asked a great question: *Do you understand what you are reading?*

The man answered, *Well, how could I, unless someone guides me?* A perfect answer! And that's exactly what we need today – Christian communicators who will *guide* others to the truth. The word *guide* is the same word used of the Spirit of God's role as described in *John 16:13*, *He will guide you into all truth*. The original concept involves leading someone down a clear path. At the heart of evangelism is one who knows the path and is able to effectively take others along the journey. That requires clearness and an understanding of where people are in order to take them to where you want them to be.

5. Living with Wisdom – The Lifestyle that Reflects the Gospel

Verse five begins with the urge to, *Conduct yourselves with wisdom*. As evangelists, our conduct must match our message. Paul understood that effective communication must be backed up by an authentic lifestyle. This lifestyle is to be applied *with wisdom*. I take that to mean a mature perspective that evaluates the implications of one's actions.

Someone once asked a mentor of mine; *Do you practice what you preach?* As a young intern watching, I was waiting to see how he would respond. Without delay, he responded, *Sir, my desire is to preach only that which I am practicing.*[48]

Effective communication must flow out of the depth of one's life. Not that we are perfect, but that, with wisdom, we are progressively maturing in our walk with Christ. But I think Paul is going one step further by implying that we live attractive, authentic lives before the non-Christian world because they are watching us. They are watching to see if our walk matches our talk.

But what is this authentic lifestyle supposed to look like? I think this "authentic lifestyle" has to do primarily with our responses to the situations of life. As I mentioned earlier, people are watching us to see if this "God thing" really relates. In *1 Peter 3:15*, Peter writes, *But sanctify Christ as Lord in your hearts, always being ready to make a defense to everyone who asks you to give an account for the hope that is in you, yet with gentleness and reverence*. Though this verse is normally used to support defending the faith against attacks from its opponents, this verse is written in a specific context. That context begins in *verse 8*, where Peter is summing up his teaching on the proper responses that we should have. One of the items he mentions is how we respond when insulted. He writes, *not returning evil for evil, or insult for insult, but giving a blessing instead; for you were called for the very purpose that you might inherit a blessing*. When we respond supernaturally to an insult by giving a blessing instead, people will take notice. They are overwhelmed and often will come back and ask you for "the reason for the hope that is in you." It is in that context that Peter writes, *Be ready to tell them*.

6. Relevant Exposure to Outsiders – Being Salt and Light in the World

The term *outsiders* occurs three other times in the New Testament (*1 Cor. 5:12, 13; 1 The. 4:12;* and *1 Tim. 3:7*). In every instance Paul uses it to refer to those outside the family of God. It is these *outsiders* with whom we are to conduct ourselves with wisdom. I have listed it as a separate point. This is because I feel it is one of the most neglected aspects of Christian communication today.

NOTES

In order for relevant exposure with outsiders to take place, Christians must come in contact with those outsiders. The principle here is one of exposure, not isolation. And yet that runs contrary to much of our modern teaching and practice.

It seems that today we fall into one of two extremes: either we are so much involved in the world's programs and ethics that no one can see a difference between us and the world, or we try to be so different and so isolated from non-believers that no one can hear what we are talking about. Studies have indicated that when someone comes to saving faith in Christ as an adult, with a large network of relationships with non-Christians, within twelve to eighteen months those relationships have ended.

There are many believers today who have no non-Christian friends at all. And yet Jesus said in *Matthew 5:13-16, You are the salt of the earth... you are the light of the world*. Salt was primarily used in those days as a preservative to counteract the decay in the meat. But the salt was ineffective unless it touched the meat. It had to have *"relevant exposure"* if it was to be effective. Rebecca Pippert's book on evangelism is entitled, *Out of the Saltshaker and Into the World*.[49] This is exactly what we ought to be about. We are to come together for worship, praise, fellowship and teaching, but then we are sent out, equipped to minister in the world (*Eph. 4:11-13*).

Jesus also used the analogy of light. One of the purposes of light coming from a lamp is to counteract the darkness. But again, the light must touch the darkness in order to remove it.

The Church today needs to learn all over again that it must encourage its members to reach out and penetrate society. We cannot transform it from a distance. If a significant part of evangelism is relationally oriented, and I believe it is, we will not effectively reach people for Christ that we do not know.

What I am suggesting is that we must take the initiative to build connections to non-Christians, learning to be comfortable with them, without compromising our standards. Impossible, you say? Then I suggest that you haven't read the Gospels lately, for Jesus ate with sinners and tax gatherers and they *gladly* welcomed Him. He felt comfortable with them and they felt comfortable with Him.

We are to engage the culture. Perhaps the most effective form of evangelism today is relational evangelism, where church members are strategically building relationships with friends, family, co-workers and acquaintances in an effort to bring them to genuine exposure to the Gospel. You can do this in your own village. You know so many people.

I think as we initiate this process, the results will spill over to our public communication. As we are comfortable with non-Christians' individually, we will be comfortable in our group communications with them. We will feel less threatened by them and less alienated from them, and, perhaps more importantly, they will feel less threatened by us and less alienated from us.

7. Making the Most of the Opportunity of the Open Door – Being Ready to Respond

The seventh dimension to effective communication Paul suggests is that we must make the most of the opportunity given to us. The phrase *making the most* suggests a purposeful strategy on our part to get the most out of the opportunities we find ourselves in.

And just what is this opportunity Paul speaks about? The word is *kairos*, which often refers to *significant time*. I take it that this opportunity is God's time, and an opportune moment for proclaiming the Gospel. We've prayed for God to open a door for the Word – and He has. Now this is our opportunity. And we must take advantage of it.

When God opens a door for us, we must not fail to go through it. We saw in our studies in *Acts* that Paul was always ready to preach the Gospel at a moment's notice. Whether it was before a king, or before a group of philosophers, in the synagogue or in the courtroom, Paul was ready.

I believe there are three essential elements to always being ready. One is being ready intellectually, knowing your material and what you believe. In Paul's case it was often his personal testimony and an apologetic for the resurrection. The second is being ready spiritually, a spiritual sensitivity to the leading of the Holy Spirit and the discernment to know what would be an appropriate manner in which to proceed. It is not only looking for the open door, but also knowing how to walk through it. That often involves knowledge of the audience. The third and final element is the boldness to accomplish the task. Timid people often let divine opportunities pass them by. But Paul wrote to a timid Church leader named Timothy in *2 Timothy 1:7*, saying, *For God has not given us a spirit of timidity, but of power and love and discipline.*

The one word constantly used to describe the preaching of the Apostles was *boldness*. I am not suggesting that only naturally outgoing people can be effective evangelists. I am simply saying that when the time comes to speak, the disciple who is characterized by a spirit of *power, love and discipline* will take advantage of the situation.

8. Gracious Conversational Speech – Meeting People One-On-One

Paul goes on to say in *verse six, Let your speech always be with grace*. This grace refers to charm and attractiveness in daily conversations. It is used in the sense to mean pleasantness, attractiveness, and charm. These are the elements that ought to characterize our speech.

The word speech here refers to daily conversation in the marketplace, not proclamation from a pulpit. The phrase in *verse three, speaking forth* the mystery of Christ, refers to a formal public delivery. But here Paul is saying that even our daily conversations should be gracious and sprinkled with pleasant charm. It is a positive spirit, an attractive personality and a polite behavior produced as the Spirit of God controls our lives. Paul described this as the *sweet aroma of the knowledge of God (2 Corinthians 2:14)*.

9. The Seasoning of Salt – Attractiveness and Relevance in our Conversations

Paul goes on to say that this conversation should be seasoned by salt. Salt was also used as a seasoning to add taste and flavor, producing zest and liveliness to the food. Our conversations should be lively and engaging. We should never be *dull* when presenting the Gospel.[50]

We ought to be passionate in our approach to others. To be sure, there will be times when we must confront and play the role of Prophet. There are strong and tough words in the Bible, and we must proclaim them honestly, but generally we ought to be attractive and charming in our approach. Please note that this is not an end in itself. We don't win people simply by being pleasant. But it is our goal to not put any stumbling blocks before people other than the necessary stumbling block of the cross of Jesus Christ.

10. Knowing How to Respond to Each Person

Paul concludes this section by saying, "so that you may know how you should respond to each person." Knowing how to respond rightly involves listening. I believe far too much effort in Christian communication is spent in talking. We need to listen far more than we do to the questions people are asking. Jesus was very much in tune with the needs of His day. We ought to be experts in where our culture is and the needs of those we are trying to reach.

1 Chronicles 12:32 says, *They understood the times in order to know what to do*. We cannot help people unless we understand the times in which we live and the effects these times are having on them. Significant issues in our culture greatly affect the attitudes and behavior of people today. We need to know what is going on in order to meet the needs of those affected by the trends of our day.

And that is exactly what Paul is suggesting in *Colossians 4*. Listen. Know how to respond to each person. These ten steps ought to be what we pray for when it comes to evangelism.

> **Assignment:**
>
> What do you pray for when you pray about evangelism? How does understanding *Colossians 4:2-6* change what you will pray for in the future?

Chapter 15
The Evangelist and the Missional Church

1. The Definition of an Evangelist

The ministry gift of the *Evangelist* is given by the Holy Spirit to women and men to preach the Gospel to unbelievers and to equip other believers to do the same, while leading the entire community of faith (to which they are connected) to expand their borders as well as plant new churches.

Ephesians 4:11 says *He gave some as evangelists*. Research that I have seen shows that this number is around *1%* of those in a congregation.[51] Identifying, training, and empowering those with that gift is vital to see the church reach its potential.

The Evangelist is the method that makes the church missional. To be missional means to be captivated and devoted to accomplishing the mission… in this case, the fulfillment of the Great Commission.

The calling of the Evangelist is to preach the Gospel and equip the saints to do the same. When an evangelist is practically connected to a local church and in a working relationship with the pastor and ministry team, there is a dynamic power released into the life of that community. When this gift is missing, the fruit of evangelism and outreach diminishes.

Imagine traveling to a foreign country and visiting the churches and noticing there were no Pastors in any congregations. There would instantly be the awareness that those churches would be lacking in a vital grace that God intended to give them through that gift. In many contexts today, this scenario is true where Evangelists are concerned. They are virtually missing from the day-to-day life of the church.

Restoring the gift of the Evangelist to the life of the local church should be a top priority for every leader that wants to have a missional congregation that impacts their community with the Gospel.

Take the example of C. H. Spurgeon. When he dedicated the Metropolitan Tabernacle in 1867, he said he desired to plant 100 churches in London, England before he died. He employed two strategies. First, he built a Pastors' College. Second, he also started an Evangelist Association that had over 100 Evangelists. These Evangelists preached in over 600 places in the city on a regular basis. Whenever there was a breakthrough, he would send in a Pastor from the college to preserve the fruit. The result? When he died in 1892, they had planted over 200 churches in London![52]

2. The Role of the Evangelist

The mistaken notion is that the Evangelist is primarily a revivalist or someone who conducts evangelistic meetings. They stir the church temporarily, yet the fruit is said to not last. However, when an Evangelist is properly functioning in the life of a church

> **NOTES**

they are helping to identify and train other evangelists that will be connected to that body of believers and providing daily encouragement and help in equipping God's people. Gospel meetings are wonderful if they are able to be a part of the Evangelist's role rather than the only thing they do.

3. The Job Description of an Evangelist:

    A. **A preacher of the Gospel** - the greatest form of evangelism is simply preaching the Gospel.

    B. **Can be male or female** - this gift is given to women as well as men. The first evangelists were the women who went to the tomb that first Easter morning. They were instructed to tell the good news to the Apostles that Christ had risen. Another example was the Samaritan woman in *John 4*. After she came to faith in Christ, she went back and told the entire region about Jesus.

    C. **Is a gatherer** - that seeks the lost and gathers them to be a part of Christ's church.

    D. **A builder** - that lays the foundations of true discipleship. They should go beyond giving an invitation and having people pray a "sinner's prayer" and make sure that Christ is fully preached and that the foundations of repentance and faith are laid.

    E. **An equipper** - the Evangelist must mentor other Evangelists as well as train believers to make disciples.

    F. **A strategist** - they can devise tools and strategies that attract the lost and enable believers to share the Gospel more effectively.

    G. **A pioneer** - they should lead the faithful beyond the church walls into the harvest field. They are able to see outreaches turn into new church plants.

Overall, the Evangelist is a vital part of any church team that desires to be missional.

Assignment:

Do you have the gift of the evangelist? If so, how has it been demonstrated in your ministry? Do you know others who have this gifting? How can you partner with them in your ministry to become more missional?

Chapter 16
What Does It Mean To Make Disciples?

Introduction

Acts 18:23 says, *After spending some time there, he (Paul) departed and went from one place to the next through the region of Galatia and Phrygia, strengthening all the disciples.*

Let's begin by defining some terms. First, what is discipleship? Simply, discipleship is the process of making disciples. We'll discuss more of this later in this chapter, but it is good to understand at the beginning that discipleship is helping someone grow and mature as a follower of Jesus.

Okay, so what is a disciple? The believers in Antioch in *Acts 11:25-26* were the first ones to be called *Christians*. Though it was initially meant as a derogatory term, meaning *Little Christs*, the name continued. Since then, followers of Jesus have primarily been known as *Christians* all over the world. Why then do we also use the word *disciple*? The word translated *disciple* can mean *student, follower and learner.* A disciple is someone who first has trusted Jesus to be his Savior. He or she has been saved by grace through faith, not because of what they have done for God, but by grace – what God has done for them.

However, it is not enough to simply know Jesus as *Savior*. We are also called to follow Him as *Lord*. It is important to note that this is not an optional phase for Christians. Just as a new baby is born into this world, that child must now grow and be nurtured by his or her parents to grow to maturity. Growth and development are not *optional* for that child. Similarly, when we come to Jesus by faith alone, we experience a *new birth* (see *John 3:1-16*). Now that we are in the faith, we must have spiritual leaders who will train us and direct us along the paths of growth. Growth and development are not optional.

Men such as Dr. Earl Radmacher feel that the evangelical world now contains the largest spiritual nursery in its history. ***It is our job as leaders to move people from infancy to the infantry.***

Assignment:

Paul talked about this exact concept in *1 Thessalonians 2:1-16*. Read these verses slowly. As you do, please notice three things:

- *verse 7*: Paul treated them like a mother would treat her own children.
- *verse 11*: He dealt with them like a father would his own children.
- *verses 12-14*: The result was that they grew to the point where they walked worthy of the Gospel and became imitators of Christ.

(Assignment continued on following page.)

NOTES

> **Assignment (continued):**
>
> Write down your observations from this passage on a separate sheet of paper. Have you ever had someone disciple you like Paul talked about here? What did they do that helped you the most? Have you ever built into someone else's life like this? How did you help them grow as new believers? Discuss.

1. Discipleship Begins with Jesus' Call

All twelve disciples were called personally by Jesus Christ. This seems to be preceded by intercession on the part of Jesus.

> *In these days he went out to the mountain to pray, and all night he continued in prayer to God. And when day came, he called his disciples and chose from them twelve, whom he named apostles: Simon, whom he named Peter, and Andrew his brother, and James and John, and Philip, and Bartholomew, and Matthew, and Thomas, and James the son of Alphaeus, and Simon who was called the Zealot, and Judas the son of James, and Judas Iscariot, who became a traitor (Luke 6:12-16).*

A. Andrew and Peter's First Encounter with Jesus (*John 1:40-42*). Andrew was a follower of John the Baptist, and was told to behold the Lamb of God. Andrew responded to Jesus' call to come, see and follow Him. Andrew invited his brother Simon Peter, who also followed Christ.

B. Andrew and Peter's Second Encounter with Jesus (*Matthew 4:18-20*): Jesus walked by Andrew and Peter as they were casting their fishermen's net into the sea. He told them, *Follow Me, and I will make you fishers of men* (v. 19).

C. James and John (*Matthew 4:21-22*). Jesus approached James and John as they were in their father Zebedee's boat, mending their nets. Jesus called to them, and they left their nets and their father, and followed Him.

D. Philip and Nathaniel (*John 1:43-51*). Jesus found Philip in Galilee and said, *Follow Me.* (*v. 43*). Philip in turn told Nathaniel to come, see and follow Christ.

E. Levi (also known as Matthew) (*Mark 2:14, Luke 5:27, Mat 9:9*). Levi was a tax collector and Jesus walked by his booth, giving him the invitation to *Follow me*.

F. The remaining disciples (*Mat. 10*) were all called at some point personally by Jesus, though we don't have a written Gospel account of these moments: Judas, Bartholomew, James the son of Alphaeus, Simon the Galilean Zealot, and Judas Iscariot, the one who betrayed Jesus.

2. Discipleship Begins with our Obedient Response to Follow Jesus

A. The disciple's response was immediate (*Mat 4:20, 22, Mark 2:14*).

B. The first disciples often left things of great importance.
- Levi (Matthew) left his place of employment, a tax collector booth.
- James and John left their jobs as fishermen.
- Peter stated that they as disciples had left *all* to follow Jesus. *Matthew 18:28-30* states, *Peter said to him, "We have left all we had to follow you!" "I tell you the truth," Jesus said to them, "no one who has left home or wife or brothers or parents or children for the sake of the Kingdom of God will fail to receive many times as much in this age and, in the age to come, eternal life."*
- The love for our family and our own lives must be much less in comparison to our love and devotion to Christ. *Luke 14:26* says, *If anyone comes to me and does not hate his own father and mother and wife and children and brothers and sisters, yes, and even his own life, he cannot be my disciple.*
- Some are not willing to forsake their lives to be Jesus' disciple:
  ▶ The rich young ruler could not part with his money and possessions. *Mark 10:22* says, *Disheartened by the saying, he went away sorrowful, for he had great possessions.*
  ▶ Some don't follow because of family and obligations (*Mat 8:22*).
  ▶ Some love their safety and comfort (*Mat 8:19-20*).
  ▶ Demas loved this present world (*2 Tim 4:10*).

C. They followed Jesus completely.
- Nothing should hinder our obedience to lay down our lives and completely surrender and follow Jesus. *Luke 14:33* says: *So therefore, any one of you who does not renounce all that he has cannot be my disciple.*

3. Discipleship Involves Walking with Jesus

A. Though it seems obvious, many discipleship "programs" lack the simplicity of merely following Christ. Instead of making disciples, many are only making converts to a specific 'faith or practice' and are baptizing people into church membership, not into the body of Jesus Christ.[53]

B. The disciples spent three years in an attitude of observation, study, obedience, and imitation.[54]

C. Walking with Jesus means to abide in Him, allowing His Word to abide in us (*Joh. 15*).

4. Discipleship Involves Living By Faith

Hebrews 11:6 tells us that without faith it is impossible to please God. The Christian life is not a list of do's and do not's. *Colossians 2:6-7* says that just as we have received Christ Jesus the Lord, (by grace through faith) we are to continue walking and growing

NOTES

in Him. *Verse 7* describes how we are firmly rooted and grounded in Jesus, and now we are growing to maturity, established in the faith and being built up in Him.

You must avoid the *lie of legalism* that says we can somehow achieve the pleasure of God by our own efforts in the flesh. Legalism says we must do certain things (keep God's commands) in our own fleshly efforts in order to be accepted by Him. THAT IS NOT THE GOSPEL! The Gospel is that Jesus paid for all of my sins – and that I am now forgiven and free to follow Him by grace through faith.

> **Assignment:**
>
> This legalism was the same trap the Galatian believers fell into in the first century. Read *Galatians 3:1-3*. They had been saved by grace through faith. Now what were they doing? Why?
>
>
>
> Now read *Galatians 5:7-25*. What did Paul encourage them to do? How is a *life lived in the flesh* different from a *life lived in the Spirit*?

We will talk more about this later when we discuss the spiritual life in more depth.

5. Discipleship Involves Obedience to Christ's Commands

Having just taught you that we are to live by faith and not by legalistically attempting to gain God's pleasure by the works of the flesh, I want to add the balance to this. Jesus *has* given us commands to obey. And the Bible tells us that we are not only to *trust* – we are also to *obey*. *John 8:31* records Jesus' words to Jews who had believed in Him: *If you hold to my teaching, you are really my disciples*.

How can you understand this balance? The heart of obedience is our motivation. Under *legalism*, *I have to obey* in order to gain God's acceptance. Under *grace, I want to obey* because I am now His child and am accepted completely. I obey (*1*) out of love for God, (*2*) according to the Word of God, and (*3*) by the power of the Holy Spirit.

6. There is not a New Testament difference between 'Christian' and 'disciple'

The word *disciple* occurs *269 times* in the New Testament. The word "Christian" is found only *3 times*, and is used to speak about disciples to discern them apart from a sect of Judaism. The New Testament is a book about disciples, by disciples, and for disciples of Jesus Christ.[55]

Many people assume discipleship is a 'higher level' of Christianity. The statement to *make disciples* is a command, not an option. There are believers who fall away from Christ and others who are very inconsistent, but His call to all of us as Christians is to Follow Him.

Christ's followers should be following Christ! Read this quote by a great Christian leader:

> *A notable heresy has come into being throughout evangelical Christian circles – the widely accepted concept that we humans can choose to accept Christ only because we need Him as Savior and that we have the right to postpone our obedience to Him as Lord as long as we want to... Salvation apart from obedience is unknown in the sacred Scriptures."*[56]

This leader understood that salvation is a free gift and that we are justified by grace alone through faith alone. However, he was emphasizing the call of Scripture for Jesus to be our God in all things. The gift of salvation is free, discipleship costs us our life. Therefore, we encourage new believers to take this free gift and apply it now by following Jesus as their God.

The Bible speaks of three aspects of salvation:
- <u>Justification</u> – we are initially and completely freed from the penalty of sin. We are forgiven and adopted into God's family.
- <u>Sanctification</u> – we are continually being freed from the power of sin in our daily lives. This transformation occurs by the indwelling power of the Spirit of God (*2 Cor. 3:18*).
- <u>Glorification</u> – we will ultimately be freed from the presence of sin in heaven.

Though justification (coming to Christ) is our beginning in the Gospel, sanctification is our walk in the Gospel and glorification is our reward in heaven for the Gospel.

7. Discipleship Means Jesus is Lord

The New Testament title for Jesus Christ is "Lord." It is used in the New Testament as the preferred title for Jesus. It places Jesus as the supreme authority:
- Of Heaven and Earth (*Act. 17:24*).
- Over all creation (*Col. 1:15-17*).
- Of fallen angels and the lake of fire (*Phi. 2:10, Rev. 20:10, 14*).
- Over all kings and lesser lords (*1 Tim. 6:14-15, Eph. 1:21*).
- Over the church (*Eph. 1:22, Col. 1:18*).

NOTES

- Over our lives:
  - ▶ Our heart, soul, mind, and strength (*Mar. 12:30*).
  - ▶ Our marriage relationships (*Eph. 5:22-25*).
  - ▶ Our finances (*1 Tim. 6:6*).
  - ▶ Our life decisions (*Mat. 6:33*).
  - ▶ Our desires and will (*Rom. 12:1-2*).

Conclusion

Discipleship is simply following Jesus. It is becoming a learner or student of His ways. It begins with heeding and obeying His call to *Come, follow Me*. It continues as we in turn make disciples who also follow, obey, and submit to Jesus as Lord. Discipleship doesn't necessarily have to be a complicated process or program. It is simple and straightforward, and critical in the Body of Jesus Christ today.

Assignment:

Read the following passages. What do they tell you about being a disciple? What do they tell you about leading, teaching and training other Christians as disciples?

Luke 14:25-35

Luke 9:57-62

2 Timothy 2:1-7

Chapter 17
Misconceptions about Discipleship

Introduction

John 6:66-70 tells us, *As a result of this many of His disciples withdrew and were not walking with Him anymore. So Jesus said to the twelve, "You do not want to go away also, do you?" Simon Peter answered Him, "Lord, to whom shall we go? You have words of eternal life. We have believed and have come to know that You are the Holy One of God." Jesus answered them, "Did I Myself not choose you, the twelve..."*

It is important that we formulate a plan for discipleship that will both honor God and His Word and also serve the specific people He has sent to build His Church. Discipleship is critical in the life of the church. Alan Hirsch said *If we fail at this point (discipleship) then we fail in all the others.*[57] Let us clarify some misconceptions about discipleship.

1. Discipleship is More Than a Program

   A. The Bible tells us to continue growing and does not suggest we can ever get to the point where we stop growing. Discipleship is a life-long process! Your training here as a church planter with TTI includes workbooks that are focused on what you need to grow as a disciple of Jesus and church planter. But your training should not stop after your courses are finished.

   B. Paul reminded the church in Philippi that even he had not arrived at a state of complete maturity: *Brethren, I do not regard myself as having laid hold of it yet; but one thing I do: forgetting what lies behind and reaching forward to what lies ahead, I press on toward the goal for the prize of the upward call of God in Christ Jesus (Philippians 3:13-14).*

2. Discipleship is Not a Production Line

   A. A production line at a factory is designed to produce great amounts of the exact same product. It is dangerous to carry this same philosophy into the discipleship process.

   B. Errors in this method of discipleship:
   • It overemphasizes results at the cost of relationships.

   Disciples cannot be mass-produced. We cannot drop people into a 'program' and see disciples emerge at the end of the production line. It takes time to make disciples. It takes individual, personal attention. It takes hours of prayer for them. It takes patience and understanding to teach them how to get into the Word of God for themselves, how to feed and nourish their souls, and by the power of the Holy Spirit how to apply the word to their lives. And it takes being an example to them of all of the above.[58]

> **NOTES**

- It underemphasizes personal spiritual growth and fruit in the lives of people, giving preference to larger, outward evidences of ministry production.

C. Certain discipleship programs may not necessarily be applicable from one culture or tribe to another. What works in one culture may not work in another one. We must focus on keeping our discipleship teachings Biblically-based, not culturally biased.

D. Jesus limited His direct influence to only twelve disciples, who in turn would go and make disciples (*Mat 28:19-20; Luke 6:12-15*).

E. Paul's method was likewise to train able men who would be qualified to also personally disciple others. This is the basis of The Timothy Initiative's ministry (*2 Tim. 2:2; 1 Cor. 11:1; 2 Tim. 3:10*).

3. Discipleship is Not Just for Beginners

A. Some people think only new converts need to be involved in the discipleship process. They reason that once you've been through a discipleship program, you do not need to learn anything else.

B. This method isolates discipleship only to those who have just recently experienced conversion and are new believers in the faith. Anyone gifted in a skill knows that to master that skill you must do so with constant practice of the basics![59]

C. Errors in this method of discipleship:
- It assumes after conversion only new believers are those in need of basic discipleship and discipline.
- It misunderstands the need for continued growth and maturity in the life of a sanctified believer.

D. Scriptural correction for this method of discipleship.
- The writer of *Hebrews* explains that those who are mature through *practice have their senses trained to discern good and evil* (5:14).
- Apollos, one who was instructed *in the way of the Lord...fervent in spirit... teaching accurately the things concerning Jesus* still needed to be taught *the way of God more accurately by Priscila and Aquila (Acts 18:25-26.)*

4. Discipleship is Not Just for Leaders

A. Some people believe that only leaders need to be discipled.

B. Scriptural correction for this method of discipleship.
- The Sanhedrin took note that the disciples were *uneducated and untrained men (and) they were amazed, and began to recognize them as having been with Jesus.* (Acts 4:13-14).
- The Scriptures exhorts all Christians to *be diligent to present yourself approved to God as a workman who does not need to be ashamed, accurately handling the word of truth (2 Tim 2:15).*

- Paul explained that we are to strive to present *every man* mature in Christ (*Col 1:28-29*).
- All Christians are disciples who are born again to spiritual life when they choose to follow Jesus.[60]
- As believers in Jesus, we must choose moment by moment to follow the Lord in all things.

5. Errors of Non-Discipleship in the Church

There are several erroneous problems when true discipleship is not a healthy dynamic in the church. These errors can slow or even prohibit true spiritual maturity.

A. Limiting grace to 'forgiveness of sins' only.
- When pastors preach grace it is imperative that they do not present a Gospel that *only* preaches the forgiveness of sins. It must promote both mercy and grace.
    - Mercy is *not getting* what we *do* deserve, i.e. God's wrath, eternal torment, judgment for our sins (*James 2:13; Rom 9:16; Eph 2:4*).
    - Grace is *getting* what we *do not* deserve, i.e. God's love, forgiveness, favor, blessings, promises, comfort, and joy (*John 1:16; Rom 3:24; Rom 6:14; 1 Cor. 15:10; Rom 8:32*).
- Discipleship and sanctification should dive deeper theologically than only teaching salvation from hell. The nature of Christ's salvation is woefully misrepresented by some present-day evangelists. He announces a Savior from hell rather than a Savior from sin. And that is why so many are fatally deceived, for there are multitudes who wish to escape the Lake of fire who have no desire to be delivered from their carnality and worldliness.[61]
- Both *saving grace* and *continuing grace* should balance the life of the believer so there is not a reliance on dead works for salvation *or* sanctification. (*Ephesians 2:8-10*) Grace provides divine enablement for all of life.[62]

B. Assuming faith is merely the agreement of religious facts
- Repentance and faith are not mental adherence to information, but becoming born again by the Spirit of God and transformed into new creations. (*John 3:3; 2 Cor. 5:17*)
- Jesus said the religious leaders knew their Bibles, but did not have an abiding relationship with the Word made Flesh. (*John 5:39-40*).

C. Equating outward religious duty with inward transformation
- A ministry 'position' does not necessarily mean one has a vibrant intimate relationship with Jesus Christ.
- Many supposed believers will remind Jesus of their outward works, to which Jesus will reply, *I never knew you; depart from Me, you who practice lawlessness*. (*Mat 7:22-23*)

D. Inviting people to follow Christ without having them count the costs.[63] The Gospel of *Luke* tells us we need to prepare as a disciple, noting the costs that will come. Again, justification is free; sanctification will cost you your life.

NOTES

Assignment:

Consider these questions about discipleship:

What is your definition of discipleship?

How will you be involved in assisting men and women in their spiritual growth?

How do you plan on organizing your method of discipleship?

Chapter 18
Discipleship: Jesus' Plan to Reach the World[64]

Introduction

Once again, read Jesus' words from *Matthew 28:19-20. Go therefore and make disciples of all the nations, baptizing them in the name of the Father and of the Son and of the Holy Spirit, teaching them to observe all things that I have commanded you. And lo, I am with you always, to the end of the age.*

Church planters should ask some difficult questions: Are our efforts really fulfilling the Great Commission? Are we seeing a growing group of dedicated people who are reaching the world for Jesus as a result of our ministry? How did Jesus model discipleship for us? Specifically, what were the basic principles that determined Jesus' ministry methods?

1. Jesus' Method was to Build *Men*

A. He was not as concerned with reaching the multitudes as He was with men whom the multitudes would want to follow after.
- John and Andrew were the first to be invited by Jesus to follow Him. (*John 1:35-40*).
- Andrew's first action as a disciple was to bring his brother, Peter, to Jesus. (*John 1:41-42*).
- Jesus found Philip the next day, and Philip in turn found Nathaniel (*John 1:43-51*).
- Soon after this Matthew was called to leave his tax collector's booth (*Mark 2:13-14; Matthew 9:9; Luke 5:27-28*).
- The rest of the disciples were called by Jesus early in His first year of ministry (*Acts 1:21-22*).
- Jesus' plan was not to impress the crowd, but to usher in a Kingdom.[65]

B. These men would be entrusted with the Gospel and would lead many others to Christ (*John 17:20*).

C. Jesus believed in spiritual multiplication. His strategy was to focus on a few individuals, rather than trying to reach the masses. As He trained them, he knew these individuals would one day reach many, many others.

D. The first duty of church leadership is to see to it that a foundation is laid in the beginning on which can be built an effective and continuing evangelistic ministry to the multitudes.[66]

> **NOTES**

2. Jesus Made a Practice of Simply Being *with* His Disciples

Though we cannot literally walk with Him today, through his Spirit, we nonetheless have been summoned by Him as well. We have been summoned to His side in order that we might be with Him, that we might really come to know Him, and that we might follow Him along the path of discipleship. But the heart of the call of Christ is to be with Him and to know Him intimately.[67]

- A. Jesus had no formal training or school or educational program for the disciples to attend or complete. There was no enrollment, no tuition, no textbooks or programs. Jesus' school and curriculum of discipleship was His life lived in closeness to His followers.

- B. Jesus' simple invitation was to *come...follow...see* (*John 1:39, 43, 46; Mark 1:17, 2:14*).

- C. Jesus' invitation was for the disciples to come be *with Him* (*1 Cor. 1:9*).

    Mark 3:14 says, *And He appointed twelve (whom he also named apostles) so that they might be with him and he might send them out to preach.*

- D. As Jesus' ministry drew to a close, He spent more time with His disciples, not less.
    - The disciples were called apart from the crowd as Jesus neared Jerusalem for the last time (*Mat. 20:17, Mark 10:32*).
    - When Jesus is in Gethsemane, His disciples close by Him (*Luke 22:41*).

- E. Jesus built into relationships with others by following up and keeping in close personal contact.
    - Jesus went to Zacchaeus' house to be with him (*Luke 19:7*).
    - When He ministered to the woman at the well in Samaria, Jesus stayed two more days in Sychar to teach the people there who believed in Him because of the woman's testimony. John adds the comment that many more believed after hearing Jesus. He modeled for the disciples what it meant to do evangelism, follow-up and discipleship (*John 4:39-42*).
    - Bartimaeus was invited to follow Jesus after He healed him of his blindness (*Mark 10:52*).
    - Women, including Mary and Martha (*Luke 10:38-42*), Mary Magdalene, Joanna, Susanna, and many others followed Jesus (*Luke 8:1-3*). These women also invested financially in Jesus' ministry. What an honor!

3. Jesus' Call Involved Obedience

- A. Jesus challenged the disciples to follow Him. To follow meant *to listen, to learn, to obey* and *to be committed to teach others also*.

- B. They were called to submit and surrender their lives to His control.
    - This involved choosing between two masters (*Luke 16:13*).
    - Old thought patterns, habits, and pleasures of the world had to now be conformed to new disciplines of the Kingdom (*Matthew 5:1-7:29, Luke 6:20-49*).

- Perfect love was now their standard of conduct (*Mat. 5:48*) that manifested itself in obedience to Jesus (*John 14:21*).
- In the same way, we are to deny self, take up our cross and follow Him (*Mark 8:34-38, 10:32-45; Mat. 16:24-26, 20:17-28; Luke 9:23-25; John 12:25-26, 13:1-20*).
- *Mark 8:34-35* says, *If anyone would come after me, let him deny himself and take up his cross and follow me. For whoever would save his life will lose it, but whoever loses his life for my sake and the Gospel's will save it.*
- To carry a cross meant the complete death of an individual to themselves and their own dreams desires and wants. We have been crucified with Christ (*Gal. 2:20*), and the old self is gone, now being raised with Christ to live a new life (*Rom. 6:1-4*).

4. Jesus Gave Himself to His Followers

A. He gave them:
- Life itself (*John 10:10*).
- All that the Father gave Him. (*John 15:15; 17:4, 8, 14*).
- Grace and truth (*John 1:17*).
- His peace, greater than that which the world gives (*John 16:33; Mat 11:28*).
- His joy in the midst of sorrow (*John 15:11; 17:13*).
- The keys to His Kingdom (*Mat. 16:19; Luke 12:32*).
- Himself, as a sacrifice and ransom for sin (*John 3:16*).

B. He showed them an example:
- Of prayer (*Luke 11:1-4; Mat 6:9-13*).
- Of using Scripture. Jesus quoted at least sixty-six Old Testament passages in speaking with the disciples. He alluded to more than ninety Old Testament references in His speaking with others.
- Of ministry. Jesus taught His disciples how to teach, by modeling it for them. He taught His disciples to care both for the individual (*John 4:1-26*) and for the multitudes (*Mat. 9:36*).

5. Jesus Gave the Disciples a Task. Then He Evaluated Their Performance

A. One of the best principles of leadership is *If you expect someone to do a task, you must inspect the work that they do.*

B. Jesus called the disciples:
- To be fishers of men (*Mat. 4:19*).
- To baptize people for repentance and into the Kingdom (*John 4:2*).
- To herald the Kingdom of God as they were sent out (*Luke 9:1; Mat. 10:1; Mark 6:7*).
- To enter cities and villages that would be receptive of the message.
- To shake the dust off their feet and leave cities that did not welcome the Good News, as a testimony against the people (*Luke 9:5*).
- To preach the Good News of the Kingdom (*Luke 9:6*).

> - To heal the sick (*Mat. 10:1*).
> - To cleanse the lepers (*Mat. 10:1*).
> - To cast out demons (*Mat. 10:1*).
> - To raise the dead (*Mat. 10:8*).
> - To undergo hardship and opposition (*Mat. 10:16*).

C. Jesus gave instruction to His disciples.
- He improved their abilities in prayer and fasting (*Mark 9:17-29; Mat. 17:14-20; Luke 9:37-43*).
- He corrected them in their theology about the Bread of Life (*Mark 16:8; Mark 8:17-19*).
- He rebuked them for their lack of grace or faith (*Luke 9:51-56; Mat. 14:30-32*).

6. Jesus Expected His Disciples to Reproduce Themselves in the Lives of Others

A. Through His Word in them, the world would come to believe in Him (*John 17:20-23*).

B. His Great Commission suggests they make disciples of all nations to the ends of the earth. (*Mark 16:15; Mat. 28:19-20; Acts 1:8*).

C. The church's witness today shows that Jesus' plan of evangelism has succeeded.

The Acts of the Apostles is the unfolding of the life of the growing Church. They lived out the principles of evangelism that Jesus taught them.[68]

Conclusion

Jesus' method was to find men whom He could give His life to. He imparted grace and truth. He consistently taught, modeled, and equipped them to be sent out to reproduce His own life and teachings in others. He sent His Spirit to them to continue the work He had begun.

Our method of discipleship can really be that simple!

Assignment:

Review the contents of this chapter. Now think about your ministry as a church planter.

What did Jesus do that you are not currently doing?

Where do you need to start to be a disciple-maker the way Jesus was?

What will be different in your church plant as you seek to follow the example of Jesus?

Chapter 19
The Disciple-Making Pastor and the Disciple-Making Church

Introduction

Jesus made it clear what He expected His early followers to do. Listen to His last words to them:

> *And Jesus came up and spoke to them, saying, All authority has been given to Me in heaven and on earth. Go therefore and make disciples of all the nations, baptizing them in the name of the Father and the Son and the Holy Spirit, teaching them to observe all that I commanded you; and lo, I am with you always, even to the end of the age (Matthew 28:18-20).*

In this passage of Scripture, Jesus gives His followers a very clear command: *to go and make disciples*. The term *disciple* is primarily a learner, or a follower.

What was on Jesus' heart for His followers? He gives them one command – and that command was not an option. He wants His followers to make disciples of all nations. So a disciple is one who listens and follows a teacher and His teachings. The term *nations* is best understood in terms of all the cultures of the world. No matter what culture is introduced to Jesus, the result is transformational.

The term *disciple* is only found in the Gospels. The epistles do not mention that word at all, but are filled with teachings on how to practice being a disciple of Jesus. So a disciple is primarily a follower of Jesus who is increasingly learning what it means to follow Him. A disciple seeks to practice His commands. A disciple is also one who is born to reproduce. We are trying to do the most difficult thing we have ever done in our lives: follow the teachings of Jesus.

1. What Does It Mean To Be A Disciple?

   A. To be a disciple means to have a teachable spirit and a heart for God.

   B. To be a disciple means to be holy – one who is set apart for God's purposes.

   C. To be a disciple means to clarify your identity. When you know *whose* you are you will understand *who* you are. In other words, belonging to Jesus gives us a new identity. He is the key to your identity.

   D. To be a disciple means to confirm your calling here on earth.

   E. To be a disciple means to manage your conflicts. When you manage your conflicts and resolve your relational difficulties, you learn more about who you are and what it means to follow Jesus.

F. To be a disciple means being able to express your personal faith. This is one of the great problems Christians have. There is nothing more effective in expressing your faith than simply living out what it means to follow Jesus.

G. To be a disciple means to build other disciples. It means to make other disciples through multiplication.

H. To be a disciple means to know Jesus better. Life is all about knowing Jesus.

In *Philippians 3:7-11*, Paul writes about what motivates him. *He says, But whatever things were gain to me, those things I have counted as loss for the sake of Christ. More than that, I count all things to be loss in view of the surpassing value of knowing Christ Jesus my Lord, for whom I have suffered the loss of all things, and count them but rubbish so that I may gain Christ, and may be found in Him, not having a righteousness of my own derived from the Law, but that which is through faith in Christ, the righteousness which comes from God on the basis of faith, that I may know Him and the power of His resurrection and the fellowship of His sufferings, being conformed to His death; in order that I may attain to the resurrection from the dead.*

Paul's goal – the driving force in His life– was to know Jesus. That was it. In the days ahead, I want to encourage you to get to know Jesus. Get to know Him by being His disciple.

2. How Do You Make Disciples?

A. Discipleship is life-on-life. You must spend time with those you wish to disciple.

It is important to note here that men should disciple other men. Women should disciple other women. See *Titus 2:2-10*.

B. You produce what you already are. You cannot take people any further than you are.

C. Follow this six step method that Jesus used:[69]
- *Tell them what* – Jesus gave the Great Commission. He told them what to do: making disciples. Making disciples involves both evangelism and discipleship. As a friend of mine says, Jesus knew nothing about evangelism without discipleship, and He knew nothing about discipleship without evangelism.
- *Tell them why* – When we follow the Great Commission we reach the world with the Gospel and build disciples to maturity.
- *Show them how* – whether preaching to large crowds or ministering one-on-one to Nicodemus or the woman at the well, Jesus showed them how to share their faith.
- *Do it with them* – Jesus encouraged the disciples to minister to others, and then evaluated their progress.
- *Let them do it* – Next, Jesus sent them out by themselves, two-by-two, for additional training in evangelism. This again was followed by critique and encouragement.

> NOTES

- *Send them out on their own* – Jesus ultimately left the ministry in the hands of the Twelve.

D. Refer to the previous chapter about how Jesus discipled His men.

3. The Disciple-Making Pastor[70]

Disciple-making exists in three primary forms: large group, one-on-one, and the small group.

A. Large group discipleship. This primarily occurs through preaching and teaching at your worship services.
- The benefit is that many people are reached, taught and discipled, at least in an introductory sense.
- The primary weakness of the large group is that it serves only to tell people what they should believe and why. It lacks the personal touch, the life-on-life aspect. The disciple-making pastor preaches and teaches Biblical principles, but it is only a start.

B. One-on-one discipleship is very effective.
- It is intensive. It is focused. And it can be the best forum for life-change and reproduction.
- The problem with one-on-one discipleship is that it takes a long time. Also, a one-on-one relationship does not take advantage of the multiple relationships that a small group provides. In a one-on-one discipleship relationship, you only learn from one person. In a small group, you learn from all those in the group.

C. Small group discipleship. A small group is made up of three to twelve participants, plus the leader. As mentioned before, all members of the group should be of the same sex. Men are part of a men's discipleship group, while women are part of a women's discipleship group.
- The small group was Jesus' example. He demonstrated the superiority of the small group for training. He ministered to the multitudes with much of His teachings. The feeding of the 5,000, the Sermon on the Mount, the parables concerning the Kingdom of God and many other large group meetings were very effective. Jesus' one-on-one encounters were also dynamic. The Gospel of John alone describes over twenty-five personal interviews. Jesus' ministry included both large groups and one-on-ones.
- At different times and phases of His ministry Jesus' followers were numbered as many as several thousand, 500, 120, 70 and the 12. But when it came to training, Jesus chose the small group as His primary method. The fact that He chose the Twelve *to be with Him* is proof of that.
- Small groups are the best environment for the pastor to build into the life of men. Skill development, prayer times, peer relationships, outreach projects and training of disciple-makers are all best done in a small group environment.
- Pastoral care can be given by the pastor to the men he has discipled. This not only follows the Biblical pattern of *Ephesians 4:11-16*, it takes an incredible burden off the pastor. Now he can be focused on developing leaders, preaching, teaching and prayer. See *Acts 6:1-6*.

4. The Disciple-Making Church[71]

A. Disciple-making is not only for every Christian. It is the job of every church.

B. The disciple-making church has five characteristics:
- In leadership... the church is led by elders leading a congregation. As you read the New Testament, notice that there was never simply a single individual who led a church. It was always led by several leaders. *Plurality of leadership* is the Biblical model. As Jesus was the main leader for the disciples, Paul was the main leader with the church planting ministry. However, Paul did not lord it over others. He relied on and needed his team of leaders.
  ▶ In *Acts 13:1-3*, the Church at Antioch had five gifted leaders.
  ▶ Titus was told to appoint *elders* (plural) in every church (*Titus 1:5*).
  ▶ Jesus always sent the disciples out two-by-two.
  ▶ Paul always had missionary companions and apprentices.
- In guidance... the church is led by gifted individuals under the control of the Holy Spirit. No one person has all the gifts. *1 Corinthians 12* says that the body has many parts and all are important. *Ephesians 4:16* talks about the Body of Christ growing *by what every (gifted individual) supplies*.
- In training... *2 Timothy 2:2* talks about gifted men equipping others. The leadership community in a church is always engaged in multi-level training.
- In outreach... a Biblical church must encourage individual evangelism (every member taking the initiative to present Christ to their network of family, friends and relationships). But the church must also be involved in evangelistic teamwork.
- In pastoral care... rather than one pastor attempting to meet all the needs of the individuals in a growing church, we need to recognize that Christ meets the needs of people through the gifts of the Body.

Assignment:

Who are you training in your church?

How are you training them?

What are you training them to do?

Chapter 20
How Jesus Discipled His Men and Prepared Them for Leadership

Introduction

I want to continue our thoughts from an earlier chapter about Jesus' plan for evangelism. In that chapter we primarily looked at the four Gospels. However, the same method continued in the book of *Acts*.

The imaginary story is told of Jesus returning from His work on earth into heaven. He visited the angels who asked Him how His time on earth went. He replied that His work was very successful. *"How many leaders did you leave behind,"* the angels asked. *"Eleven!"* replied Jesus, triumphantly. *"Only eleven? Is that all? What if they fail? What if they don't build the church? What is your other plan?"* the angels asked. *"I have no other plan. I am depending on them."*

In the first fourteen verses of *Acts 1* there are incredible insights into how Jesus discipled the Apostles and how He prepared them for leadership in His Church.

1. He Modeled Life and Ministry for Them – *v. 1*

"All that Jesus began to do and teach…"

He prepared them by what He did. One of the key principles of ministry is that *Discipleship is caught, not taught*. Be consistent in your own Bible study. Pray with the men you are discipling. Be an example to them.

2. He Taught Them God's Truth – *v. 1*

"To teach" means to impart a specific body of truth. Jesus had a plan to teach His men. He knew specifically what He wanted to teach them. He taught them about the Kingdom (*v. 3*). He taught the promises of God to them (*v. 4*). He taught the ministry of the Holy Spirit (*v. 5, 8*). He taught them His purposes and objective: to reach the world with the Gospel (*v. 8*).

3. By working – *v. 2*

He worked with them until the very last day. In *John 17:4* Jesus says, *I have finished the work which You have given Me to do*. Part of the work the Father had given Him was to disciple His men. We work until He calls us home

4. By giving orders – *v. 2, 4*

Give people direction. People need to be told what to do. You must understand the various cultural differences and live out what it means to be a servant leader. But don't back away from giving people direction. How do you do that? Be committed to Jesus so much that people are compelled to follow Him!

5. By living filled with the Spirit – *v. 2*

This is the basis of all that we do. The Spirit of God must fill (control, direct and empower) our lives on a moment by moment basis. See *Ephesians 5:18*.

6. By being available – *v. 3*

Are you available to people? If you are fully committed to the Lord you will be fully committed to people. *Acts 1:3* says that Jesus *presented Himself alive* to the believers. He revealed Himself to them. The question you must ask is: have I made a total once for all final commitment to other people? How can you best serve them?

7. By showing them God's life – *v. 3*

He was *alive*. Let people see Jesus Christ in your life. They might read about what a Spirit-filled Christian is in a book. But what will attract them to God's life is to see it lived out in you!

8. By the resurrection and appearances – *v. 3*

It took 40 days to prove to the disciples that He was alive – *"by many convincing proofs."* Prove to others that Jesus is alive in you by ministering sacrificially and giving generously to them. Be a servant – that will attract them to Him.

9. By building expectations – *v. 4, 5*

He told them to wait, which means to be in expectation about something that is going to happen. You must live life expectantly, knowing God is going to do something in your life

10. By making them into a team – *v. 4*

The key word here is *"together"* – prepare people together. In the Gospels, Jesus did not spend time alone with any one disciple. He spent time with the GROUP of disciples. He even rebuked Peter in front of the entire group. Minister to people in small groups.

11. By letting them ask questions – *v. 6*

People want to learn. Welcome their questions and be patient in answering them.

12. By refocusing their attention – *v. 7, 8*

The disciples were pre-occupied with the Kingdom and when the Second Coming was going to occur. He straightened out their wrong thought patters and focused on the purpose at hand. He told them, they were thinking incorrectly.

NOTES

13. By casting a vision for the world – *v. 8*

Through this passage we understand that the most important thing in Jesus' mind was reaching the world with the Gospel. That's what He taught them.

14. By giving them a strategy – *v. 8*

He taught them how to reach the world with the Gospel. He gave them the strategy of going from Jerusalem to Judea and Samaria and ultimately to the entire world.

15. By sending the Holy Spirit to help – *v. 9-11*

In *Acts 2* we read about how the Holy Spirit descended on the disciples at Pentecost and empowered them to serve and witness. Jesus promised here to send them the Spirit to help them in their witnessing.

16. By allowing them to participate in what was most important to Him – *v. 8-11*

Reaching the world was Jesus' ultimate goal. He enlisted them to follow and give their lives to that cause. He came to give His life a ransom for many, that millions could have eternal life. Recruit others to follow you as you follow Jesus.

Chapter 21
Growing Disciples to Maturity (Understanding the Basics of the Spiritual Life)

Introduction

In this chapter I am going to define for you what the Christian life is all about. You will want to apply these teachings to your life – and you will want to help those you train and disciple to learn and live by them as well.

This definition will have five parts to it. And each one of them will build on the previous points.

1. The Christian Life is the Life of Christ

There is a difference between Christianity and every other religion of the world. All other religions say do this and you will be accepted by God. Christianity says: *here is what Jesus has done for you. Now live!*

Galatians 2:20 states, *I have been crucified with Christ; it is no longer I who live, but Christ lives in me.* It is never our self-effort … but it is the Savior's life lived through us.

2. The Christian Life is the Life of Christ Reproduced in the Believer

The whole verse in *Galatians 2:20* says, *I have been crucified with Christ; it is no longer I who live, but Christ lives in me; and the life which I now live in the flesh I live by faith in the Son of God, who loved me and gave Himself for me.* The Christian life is not a life lived for God, but the life of God lived in us, through us, with us, and sometimes in spite of us by the power of the Holy Spirit.

3. The Christian Life is the Life of Christ Reproduced in the Believer by the Power of the Holy Spirit

On the night before His crucifixion, Jesus told the disciples *I will pray the Father, and He will give you another Helper, that He may abide with you forever – the Spirit of truth, whom the world cannot receive, because it neither sees Him nor knows Him; but you know Him, for He dwells with you and will be in you. I will not leave you orphans; I will come to you (John 14:16-18).*

When the Spirit of God fills and empowers our lives on a daily basis (*Eph. 5:18*), the natural result will be that the fruit of the Spirit will be produced through our lives. *Gal. 5:22-23* lists that fruit: *love, joy, peace, longsuffering, kindness, goodness, faithfulness, gentleness, self-control.*

4. The Christian Life is the Life of Christ Reproduced in the Believer by the Power of the Holy Spirit According to the Word of God

We are called to live according to truth. God's Word is truth (*John 17:17*). Jesus Himself said that *man should not live by bread alone, but by every word that proceeds from the mouth of God* (*Matthew 4:4*).

I love the way Paul wrote it in *Colossians 3:16* – *Let the word of Christ dwell in you richly. In all wisdom, teaching and admonishing one another in psalms and hymns and spiritual songs, singing with grace in your hearts to the Lord.* Real spiritual growth begins to take place when the Word of God dwells richly in the lives of His followers.

5. The Christian Life is the Life of Christ Reproduced in the Believer by the Power of the Holy Spirit According to the Word of God Lived out in Faith and Obedience

Jesus told His disciples, *He who has My commandments and keeps them, it is he who loves Me. And he who loves Me will be loved by My Father, and I will love him and manifest Myself to him* (*John 14:21*).

Let me highlight four specific areas where we must be obedient to the Lord Jesus Christ.

A. Prayer and Worship. We must spend daily time praying. The church of Jesus is built by the prayers of His believers.

B. Truth-telling. We are called to *speak truth to one another* (*Eph. 4:25*). This means we must not lie in any area. We cannot give exaggerated statistics. We cannot deliberately mis-lead people, even if we think we are doing so with good intentions. Jesus wants us to honor Him by telling the truth at all times.

C. Sexual Purity. One area where everyone struggles is in remaining sexually pure. The act of sex is reserved for marriage only (*Heb. 13:4*). We must maintain pure and proper contact with members of the opposite sex. We must also maintain pure thoughts, for Jesus said to look on a woman lustfully is the same as committing adultery with her (*Mat. 5:27-28*).

D. Trusting God for our Daily Needs. *Matthew 6:25-34* has some great words for every believer. We must not worry, but rather trust God for our daily needs. It is wrong for us to desire more than God has provided for us. Read this passage slowly and ask Jesus to make you a person who trusts Him with money and financial security.

Therefore I say to you, do not worry about your life, what you will eat or what you will drink; nor about your body, what you will put on. Is not life more than food and the body more than clothing? Look at the birds of the air, for they neither sow nor reap nor gather into barns; yet your heavenly Father feeds them. Are you not of more value than they? Which of you by worrying can add one cubit to his stature? So why do you worry about clothing? Consider the lilies of the field, how they grow – they neither toil nor spin, and yet I say to you that even Solomon in all his glory was not arrayed like one of these. Now if God so clothes the grass of the field, which today is, and tomorrow is thrown into the oven, will He not much more clothe you, O you of little faith? Therefore do not worry, saying 'What shall we eat?' or 'What shall we drink?' or 'What shall we wear?' For after all these things the Gentiles seek. For your heavenly Father knows that you need all these things. But seek first the Kingdom of God and His righteousness, and all these things shall be added to you. Therefore do not worry about tomorrow, for tomorrow will worry about its own things. Sufficient for the day is its own trouble.

Assignment:

In what areas are you not obeying God right now? Where do you need to repent and change, trusting Him and obeying Him in every area of your life?

Now that you have a good definition of the Christian life, how will you disciple and train others to live the Christian life more effectively? What will your church be known for?

Chapter 22
Applying the Basics of Discipleship

Introduction

In this chapter, I would like to introduce you to some basic concepts of discipleship. What are the *basic principles* someone needs to know as a new believer? To do that, I am going to use several illustrations used by the Navigators (a world-wide discipleship ministry) for more than fifty years.

1. The Wheel Diagram – Growing as a Christian

The first diagram is the Wheel diagram.[72] This simple but effective illustration helps Christians understand what they are called to do as disciples of Christ. Each part of this illustration represents an important factor of a Christian life. Use this illustration to gain understanding about important spiritual disciplines in your own life. What areas encourage you? What areas challenge you?

You can also sketch out "The Wheel Illustration" on a napkin or scrap of paper with someone you are discipling. Help challenge them to think clearly about how to be an obedient follower of Christ.

    A. The Hub: Christ the Center

    2 Corinthians 5:17- Therefore if anyone is in Christ, he is a new creation; old things have passed away; behold, all things have become new.

    Galatians 2:20 – I have been crucified with Christ; it is no longer I who live, but Christ lives in me; and the life which I now life in the flesh I live by faith in the Son of God, who loved me and gave Himself for me.

    Making Christ central in your life is an act of your will. Surrendering totally to Christ's authority and lordship may be at conversion or after some months or even years. God creates within you the desire to do what He wants you to do in order to express His lordship in your life.

B. The Rim of the Wheel: Obedience to Christ

Romans 12:1 - I beseech you therefore, brethren, by the mercies of God, that you present your bodies a living sacrifice, holy, acceptable to God, which is your reasonable service.

John 14:21 – He who has My commandments and keeps them, it is he who loves Me. And he who loves Me will be loved by My Father, and I will love him and manifest Myself to him.

Some acts of obedience to God are internal. But even these internal acts of obedience, such as attitudes, habits, motives, sense of values, and day-to-day thoughts, eventually come up in relationships with other people. The proof of your love for God is your demonstrated obedience to Him.

C. The Vertical Dimension: How You Relate to God

- The Bible Spoke

2 Timothy 3:16 – All Scripture is given by inspiration of God, and is profitable for doctrine, for reproof, for correction, for instruction in righteousness.

Joshua 1:8 – This Book of the Law shall not depart from your mouth, but you shall meditate in it day and night, that you may observe to do according to all that is written in it. For then you will make your way prosperous, and then you will have good success.

As God speaks to you through the Scriptures, you can see His principles for life and ministry, learn how to obey, and become acquainted with the Christ who is worthy of your unqualified allegiance. A vital personal intake of God's Word is essential for health and growth.

- The Prayer Spoke

John 15:7 – If you abide in Me, and My words abide in you, you will ask what you desire, and it shall be done for you.

Philippians 4:6-7 – Be anxious for nothing, but in everything by prayer and supplication, with thanksgiving, let your requests be made known to God; and the peace of God, which surpasses all understanding, will guard your hearts and minds through Christ Jesus.

Prayer is a natural response to God as you hear Him speak to you through His Word. It is sharing your heart with the One who longs for your companionship and who cares about your concerns. Prayer unleashes the power of God in your personal battles and in the lives of those for whom you pray.

D. The Horizontal Dimension: How You Relate to Others

- The Fellowship Spoke

    Matthew 18:20 – For where two or three are gathered together in My name, I am there in the midst of them.

    Hebrews 10:24-25 – And let us consider one another in order to stir up love and good works, not forsaking the assembling of ourselves together, as is the manner of some, but exhorting one another, and so much the more as you see the Day approaching.

    Learning from and encouraging others creates a unity pleasing to God. God has directed Christians to build each other up through inter-dependence and loving relationships with each other.

- The Witnessing Spoke

    Matthew 4:19 – Follow Me, and I will make you fishers of men.

    Romans 1:16 – For I am not ashamed of the Gospel of Christ, for it is the power of God to salvation for everyone who believes, for the Jew first and also for the Greek.

    The natural overflow of a rich vibrant life in Christ should be sharing with others how they too can have this life. God has given believers the privilege and responsibility of reaching the world with the Good News about Christ.

2. The Hand Diagram – The Importance of the Bible

Early in my journey with Jesus, I learned another simple illustration from the Navigators ministry that has helped me relate to the Bible. You can use this illustration to teach new believers how they must value God's Word. Even if they don't have a copy of the Bible for themselves, it is important that they grasp the principles behind this illustration.

Picture a hand holding the Bible... each finger labeled as follows:

> NOTES

A. First, we are to *Hear* the Bible as it is being taught. *Romans 10:17* says that *"faith comes by hearing, and hearing by the Word of God."*

B. Second, we are to *Read* the Bible. *Revelation 1:3* promises a special blessing to those who read its words.

C. Third, we are to *Study* the Bible. The Berean Church in *Acts 17:11 "received the word with all readiness, and searched the Scriptures daily."* That's a good model for us today.

D. Fourth, we are to *Memorize* the Bible. *Deuteronomy 6:6-7* states, *"And these words which I command you today shall be in your heart. You shall teach them diligently to your children, and shall talk of them when you sit in your house, and when you walk by the way, and when you lie down and when you rise up."*

E. Finally, we are to *Meditate* on the Bible. The first Psalm says that we should *"meditate on the law day and night."* That means to think it over, to dwell on it, to look at it from different perspective... and always let it be the guiding force in our lives.

What is the point? When you have all five fingers in action, you have a firm grasp on the Bible. And when you have a firm grasp on the Bible, it has a firm grasp on your life!

Assignment:

Remember and try to explain these two illustrations to a partner. Identify two or three young converts who you can sit down with this week and present these illustrations to them. This will begin the process of discipleship for you. After this, you can take them through the *Disciple Making Disciples* material in the Appendix of this book.

Appendix 1:
Disciple Making Disciples

Lesson 1 – The Assurance of Salvation

Congratulations, you have been born into God's family. You are a child of God. From now on you have a new relationship with God and you can receive all of His promises.

1. Let us review how we receive eternal life through Jesus.

    A. What is the result of sin? (*Isaiah 59:2*)

        _____

        _____

    B. People try many different ways to find God yet fail, why? (*Ephesians 2:8-9*)

        _____

        _____

    C. How does God draw us to Himself? (*1 Peter 3:18*)

        _____

        _____

2. The way of salvation

    A. <u>The redemption of Jesus + your faith + repentance = salvation</u>

       Has God done what He wants to do (death & resurrection?)
       _____ yes   _____ no

       If you have 'believed then you are saved!

    B. What does Jesus promise to those who follow Him? (*John 10:28*) _____

    C. Eternal life does not only mean that you will live forever; this life with God also means that we are able to live a life of holiness, righteousness, kindness, and strength. We will forever receive the blessings of God.

    D. Believing in Christ not only means you will have eternal life, but starting right now, you have a new life, letting you feel peace, happiness, and blessings at this very moment. You will also live to bless others.

3. **Your response.**

    Do you know you have been saved? _____ yes _____ no

    Do you know you have received eternal life? _____ yes _____ no

    Possible Conclusions (circle one)
    - I have been saved
    - I haven't been saved
    - I still don't know.

4. **If anyone is in Christ, he is a _____,
    the old _____, the new has come.** (*2 Cor. 5:17*)

    A. The saved will be changed. Have you experienced the following changes?
    _____ inner peace
    _____ awareness of sin
    _____ constantly feel God's love
    _____ ability to defeat sin
    _____ peace of having been forgiven
    _____ desire to read Bible
    _____ attitude of becoming better
    _____ caring for others

5. **If you sin again, are you still saved?** (*1 John 1:9*)

6. **Please joyfully fill in your spiritual "birth certificate."**

    On _____ (year) _____ (month) _____ (day)

    I received Jesus into my heart to be my savior. He forgave my sin, became by Lord, and took control of my life. I have become a child of God, and I am a new creation. I have begun a new life.

    Signature: _____

7. **Memorize Bible verses.**

    "He who has the Son has life, he who does not have the Son, does not have life," (*John 5:12*)

8. **When you receive this great salvation your life is full of joy and peace! The first thing that you should do is to share this good news with those around you. Tell at least *five* people everything that you have heard and learned today. In addition, train these individuals to share and train others. In the following weeks continue to teach at least *five* more individuals. This is great news and it is God's will; He is willing for all to receive salvation.**

NOTES

Lesson 2 – Understanding Prayer

Prayer is "talking" with God. When you pray you should be clear and sincere, just as the Bible records how Jesus "talked" with God and taught His disciples.

1. **Why do we need to pray?**

    A. This is God's command:
    "You should _____ pray." (Luke 18:1)

    "And pray in the Spirit, _____."
    (Eph. 6:18)

    B. This is your need:
    You can (1 Peter 5:7) _____

    To Seek God's leading:
    "If you call upon Me, I will show you great and mighty things which you do not know."
    (Jer. 33:3) _____

    To receive mercy and find grace in your time of need.
    (Heb. 4:16) _____

    C. For what things do you need to pray?
    "Do not be anxious about anything, but in _____ by prayer and petition, with thanksgiving, present your _____ to God. And the peace of God, which transcends all understanding, will guard your hearts and your minds in Christ Jesus." (Phi. 4:6-7)

2. **The content of prayer**

    Please draw a line between the verse and the correct description of prayer.

<u>Praise</u>: praise God's nature	1 Joh. 1:9
<u>Thanksgiving</u>: thank God for His grace	Phil. 4:6-7
<u>Ask</u>: ask God to meet your own needs	Psa. 135:3
<u>Intercession</u>: ask God to meet the needs of others	1 Thess. 5:18
<u>Confession</u>: ask God to forgive your sins	1 Tim. 2:1

3. **Three answers to prayer.**

    A. Yes (green light), you can proceed.

    B. No (red light), you cannot proceed.

    C. Wait (yellow light), God does not respond, you must be patient.

4. **The Three-Fold Will of God**

   A. What God has commanded us to do – This is what God has already determined; it can never be changed by what or how a person prays.

   B. What God allows – Sometimes, because a person pleads with God, He will allow us to receive something, but we must take responsibility for what we receive.

   C. What is pleasing to God – (*Rom. 12:2*)

5. **Attitudes of prayer**

Attitude:	Verse:
A. Have faith...	*But when he asks, he must believe and not doubt…" (James 1:6)*
B. Have the right motivation...	*"You do not have, because you do not ask God. When you ask, you do not receive, because you ask with the wrong motives." (James. 4:2-3)*
C. Confess our sins...	*"If I cherish sin in my heart, the Lord would not have listened." (Ps. 66:18)*
D. Ask according to His will...	*"This is the confidence we have in approaching God: that if we ask anything according to His will He hears us." (1 Joh. 5:14)*
E. Pray with a faithful heart...	*"That... they should always pray and not give up." (Luke 18:1)*

6. **Helps for Effective Prayer:**

   A. A disciple needs to pray *"in Jesus' name,"* (*Joh. 14:13*) because only through Jesus can a person come before God (*Joh. 14:6*)

   B. Ending our prayer with "Amen" means praying with one's true heart.

   C. Prayer has many parts: praise, thanksgiving, requests, intercession, and confession. We should not favor any part: i.e. one should not offer requests and not praise, or only requests for one's self and not others.

   D. Pray in a natural and understandable manner; avoid babbling.

   E. One can pray at any time of the day and at any place. There is no limit on the time and place of prayer.

> **NOTES**

Lesson 3 – Daily Devotions

To really know a person you need to have regular contact with that person. In the same way, if you want to have a close relationship with God, you need to "set a time" just for God daily. We need to "make a date with God" for a daily devotional.

1. The content of our devotional time

    A. Talk with God through prayer

    B. Let God speak to you through reading the Bible

2. The purpose of our devotional time

    A. To worship God – God have me!

    B. To fellowship with God – We share our concerns.

    C. To be led by God – To know His will.

3. The attitude of our devotional time

    A. What attitude does the psalmist have toward God?

    (Ps. 42:1-2) _____

    _____

    (Ps. 119:147-148) _____

    _____

4. Examples from the Bible

How did the characters in the Bible seek and know God?

Verse:	Character:	Time:	Activity:
Gen. 19:27	Abraham	Morning	Met God
Ps. 5:3			
Daniel 6:10			
Mark 1:35			

From the previous examples listed, what applications can you make to your life in terms of spending time with God?

_____

_____

5. Suggestions and tools for your spiritual life:

   A. <u>Bible</u>: Write down the Scripture; read and then write down what you learned from the reading. Meditate on the verse. Remember that you can't change what the Bible says, but you can write how it impacts your life. Although there are many good devotional books, not one can replace the Bible. The Bible is the answer to four big questions. Where do I come from? Why do I exist? How should I live? Where will I go in the future?

   B. <u>Pen & Notebook</u>: Write down your thoughts; write down what you sense God saying to you during your devotional time. *"And you shall remember all the ways which the Lord your God has led you"* (*Deu. 8:2*). You can also write down the names and needs of those you are praying for. Also note the matters that have been answered to encourage yourself.

   C. <u>Place</u>: Choose a place where you can meet with God without being disturbed. God wants you to concentrate when facing Him.

   D. <u>Time</u>: Find the most appropriate time where you can consistently meet with God.

   E. <u>Plan</u>: Choose a book in the Bible to read at your own rate, then meditate, record, pray and obey.

6. Getting ready to meet with God

   <u>Pray</u>: *"Open my eyes that I may see wonderful things in your law."* (*Ps. 119:18*)

   <u>Prepare</u>: Collect the things you need and find a quiet place. Prepare your heart, wait on God. Confess your sins

   <u>Seek God</u>: Carefully read a verse or Scripture portion. Meditate on how it relates to you. Talk with God about what you read. Pray over each item listed above.

   <u>Follow Through</u>: Obey what God reveals to you. Share with others what you have learned.

7. Keep your Devotional Life

Be faithful in keeping your daily devotion. Persevere in keeping your daily devotions; make the time a part of your daily life.

    A. It is your decision to daily meet with God. If you keep a daily time with God, you will find that you will grow in your spiritual life.

    B. While Jesus was on this earth He said, *"But seek first His Kingdom and His righteousness."* (*Mat. 6:33*) In all the things that you encounter in this world, there is nothing that is more important than you being with God.

    C. One of God's goals is for you to have fellowship with Him and to know Him. Your goal should be to praise and worship God. Although devotions will bring you many good feelings, new insights and many blessings, the main purpose of doing devotions is to know and worship God.

8. Your Commitment

Are you willing to commit to a daily devotion?

Signature _____

Beginning Date: _____

Time: _____

Place: _____

Plan: _____

_____

_____

_____

Lesson 4 – Life in the Church

When you become a Christian, you are a member of God's family. God is your heavenly Father, and all Christians are like brothers and sisters of the same family. *"... this household is the church of the living God..."* (*1 Tim. 3:15*). A household is not a building, and the "church" is not a place of worship, the church is a body of believers.

1. How does the Bible describe the relationship between Jesus and Christians?

    A. (*Rom. 12:5*) _____

    _____

    _____

    B. (*Eph. 1:22-23*)_____

    _____

    _____

2. What is the position of Christ in the church?

    A. (*Eph. 5:23*) _____

3. The Functions of the Church

The Functions of the Church	*Your Needs*
Worship: "_____God, sing to the Lord a new song, His praise in the assembly of the saints." (*Psa. 149:1*)	**To worship**
Fellowship: "And let us consider how we may spur _____ on toward love & good deeds." (*Heb. 10:24*)	**To share**
Teaching: "and teaching them to obey everything I have commanded you…" (*Mt. 28:20*)	**To learn**
Ministry: "to prepare God's people so that they body of Christ may be built up." (*Eph. 4:12*)	**To serve**
Spirit-Filled Evangelism: "But you will receive power when the Holy Spirit has come upon you…" (*Acts 1:8*)	**To spread the Gospel**

> **NOTES**

4. **Can Christians today continually not attend church?**
   ____ yes   ____ no   ____ It depends

   Do you have difficulty attending church? _____

5. **Why should you attend church?**

   A. Because we need worship, fellowship, teaching, discipline, and the Holy Spirit's power.

   B. Because this is God's command: *"Let us not give up meeting together, as some are in the habit of doing, but let us encourage one another—and all the more as you see the Day approaching."* (Heb. 10:25)

   C. To avoid deviating from the truth of the Bible.

   D. Because there are mature Christians in church to help you.

6. **Obligations we have in church**

   A. Our Obligation to profess our union with Christ – Baptism
      (*Rom. 6:1-14, Acts 2:41*)
      - Baptism is a proclamation of our faith.
        ▶ The words and actions of baptism communicate to those present that we are positioned in Christ Jesus. (*Rom. 6:3*)
      - Baptism is a confirmation of our faith.
        ▶ We know and feel that we are freed from the old dead person, and now live a new life in resurrection power. (*Rom. 6:6-14*)
      - Baptism is a witness of our faith.
        ▶ *We were therefore _____ through baptism into death in order that, just as Christ was _____ through the glory of the Father we too may live a new life. If we have been _____ like this in his death, we will certainly also be united with him _____.* (*Rom. 6:4-5*)
      - Baptism is a symbol of our faith.
        ▶ Baptism does not have the power to forgive sin. We are saved when we confess with our mouth and believe in our heart. (*Rom. 10:9*)

   B. Our Obligation to Remember – the Lord's Supper
      - Jesus personally set this as a remembrance of His death and shed blood for our sin (*Mat. 26:17-19, 26-30*).
      - When we receive the Lord's Supper, we must remember and give thanks. *"But he was _____ for our _____; he was _____ for our _____"* (*Isaiah 53:5*).
      - When we receive the Lord's Supper, it is a time to examine our actions and faith. (*1 Cor. 11:23-29*)

C. Our Obligation to Give – Offerings

Offerings are "thank you gifts" given to God and acts of worship unto God. Offerings can include sacrifices of a person's life, goals, time, abilities, and finances.

Monetary offerings are required by God and a test of the disciple's faith, love, and obedience. There are three kinds of monetary offerings:
- Tithes
  God commanded His people in the Old Testament to tithe, telling them the tithe belongs to God. The tithe was actually not an offering, but what they were required to give. (*Lev. 27:30-31*) (See *Malachi 3:8-9*).
- Gifts & Offerings
  This is a true offering, arising from a thankful and sincere heart. The amount of the gift is your own personal decision. We cannot worship God without gifts and offerings. We should not continually come empty-handed into God's presence.
- Love Offerings
  This is an offering given to others. It is motivated by love and is given according to what a person has and according to the needs of others.

> **NOTES**

Lesson 5 – God is the Heavenly Father

Jesus taught his disciples to say, *"Our father who are in heaven."* The Bible teaches us that God is our Father. He loves, protects, and disciplines His children.

1. The Heavenly Father's Love

"The Lord appeared to them from afar saying, 'I have _____ you with an everlasting love,' therefore I have drawn you with loving-kindness." (Jer. 31:3)

A. Why did God save you?
   __because you are so bad?   __because you first loved Him?
   __because you have bad luck?   __because _____

B. How does God reveal His love to you? Please write an example below.

_____

(1 John 3:1) _____

_____

_____

C. In Luke 15:11-14, Jesus talks about how a father loved his son. What similarities are there between this father and God our Father?

_____

_____

_____

2. The Heavenly Father's Protection

"But the Lord is faithful, and He will _____ you from the evil one." (2 Thess. 3:3)

A. In *Ps. 34:7*, what does God promise?

_____

B. How did God protect Elijah? (*2 Kings 6:15-18*)

_____

C. How did God protect Daniel's three friends? (*Dan. 3*)

_____

_____

D. How does God protect you when you face temptation? (*1 Cor. 10:13*)

_____

_____

3. The Heavenly Father's Provision

"And my God will _____ _____ _____ _____ according to His glorious riches in Christ Jesus." (Phi. 4:19)

A. Why are God's children not to worry? (*Mat. 6:31-32*)

_____

_____

B. What gift has God given His children to demonstrate that He is willing to meet our needs? (*Rom. 8:32*)

_____

_____

4. The Heavenly Father's Discipline

"Because the Lord _____ those He loves, and He punishes everyone He accepts as a son." (Heb. 12:6-7)

A. What are God's expectations for His children? (*Eph. 4:13*)

_____

_____

NOTES

B. How does God discipline His children?

▶ Through Friends: (*Pro. 27:17*)

_____

▶ Through the Bible: (*2 Tim. 3:16*)

_____

▶ Through Trials: (*James 1:2-4*)

_____

Which aspect of God is most meaningful to you?

__ His love & kindness

__ His provision for your needs

__ His discipline

__ His protection

Lesson 6 – Spreading the Gospel

You are now a Christian; you are a child of God and a member of God's family. You have assurance of salvation. You can pray directly to God and have fellowship with Him at any time, and you spend devotional time with Him. You are a member of His church, a blessed people. The most important thing now is that God calls you to spread the Gospel and teach them to obey all of His ways, and that they then proceed to teach even more people the good news of salvation.

1. There are four types of calls to share the Gospel:

    A. **The Call from Above**: the commandment of the Lord Jesus. (*Mark 16:15*)

    B. **The Call from Hell**: the rich man's plea to share the Gospel with his family. (*Luke 16:27-28*)

    C. **The Call from Within**: Paul was under compulsion to spread the Gospel. (*2 Cor. 5:14-15, 18-20*)

    D. **The Call from Without**: Paul heard the call from Macedonia to come. (*Acts 16:9*)

NOTES

Today each Christian should listen to the calls in their life and respond immediately.

2. We should not only lead people to become Christians, but also to become a successful "trainer" who trains others.

In this way you can rapidly spread the Gospel. (*2 Tim. 2:2*)

_____

_____

3. God's desire is for every Christian to share the Gospel with his neighbors.

He will also lead many to begin their own new small group! (*Acts 2:46-47*)

_____

_____

You should immediately respond to God and pray for the body of Christ.
Your life will be a blessing:
- By leading people to believe in the Lord.
- By starting new small groups (at your own home or any place).
- By training trainers.

The Simple and Lasting Guide to Bible Study

Once a new believer understands and completes the six basic lessons of faith, we should immediately teach them the most important factor in training a small group: "The Simple and Lasting Guide to Bible Study."

Whenever you teach or interpret the Bible for them, they can receive and learn. Yet most of these new believers will rely only on your output. They do not know how to receive the light, the blessing and the grace of God by themselves. Therefore, we must teach them a simple but lasting way to study the Bible. This will not only enable them to sustain their own personal Bible Study, but it will also give then the capability of holding and leading Bible Study groups and allowing those in the Bible study group to do the same.

There are many Bible study books and guides on spiritual growth. But most of these books do not help Christians understand how to study the Bible, how to discover the truth of God, and how to obey the truth that God has revealed to them. In reality, there are no spiritual or Bible study guides that can replace God's Word. A person can only receive God's teaching and power directly from His Word. In this way, God teaches us to trust and obey His Word. This is the most important learning. This is why we need to ask the light of the Holy Spirit to shine upon us and to guide us in spiritual growth.

Below are three important questions we must bear in mind each time we study the Bible:

1. What is the Scripture about?

2. What did the Holy Spirit speak to me today through the Scripture – what should I do to obey God's Word to me?

3. How should I teach others the truth I received from the Scripture today?

End Notes

[1] The verses I claimed during this time were *Ephesians 3:20-21*, praying that God would do exceedingly abundantly beyond anything I could ever ask or think. And He did!

[2] This chapter may sound familiar to those of you who have completed the course in Homiletics. One of the sample sermons in the appendix of that book has been expanded into the contents of this chapter.

[3] In the original Greek language of the Bible, the phrase *Go into all the world* is more accurately translated as a participle: *As you go*, or *As you are going into all the world*. The main verb in the passage is the command *Make disciples*. The three participles (*going, baptizing, and teaching*) all relate to the process of making disciples.

[4] Tim Keller, *Church Planting*, Redeemer Presbyterian Church White Paper, 2002, p. 1.

[5] C. Peter Wagner, *Strategies for Growth*, Glendale: Regal, 1987, p. 168.

[6] Lyle Schaller, quoted in D. McGavran and G. Hunter, *Church Growth: Strategies that Work* (Nashville: Abingdon, 1980), p. 100.

[7] See C. Kirk Harsdaway, *New Churches and Church Growth in the Southern Baptist Convention* (Nashville: Broadman, 1987.)

[8] Lyle Schaller, *44 Questions for Church Planters* (Nashville: Abingdon, 1991), p.12.

[9] Tim Keller, *Church Planting*, Redeemer Presbyterian Church White Paper, 2002, p. 4.

[10] The contents of this chapter are greatly expanded in the Resource CD, *Five Stages for Multiplying Healthy Churches*, by Greg Kappas and Henry Oursler, available from Grace Global Network. See www.GraceGlobalNetwork.org for information on purchasing this resource.

[11] Steve Addison, *Movements That Change the World* (Missional Press, 2009), Kindle version, Location 187ff.

[12] Ibid.

[13] Ibid.

[14] Ibid.

[15] Ibid

[16] Ibid.

[17] Alvin Reid, *Advance: Movements That Changed The World*, e-book, p. 22-24, alvinreid.com

[18] David Garrison, *Church Planting Movements Around the World Today*, WIGTake Resources, PowerPoint Presentation, 2010.

[19] Ibid.

[20] Barrett and Johnson, "World Religious Statistics," in the January 29, 2010 International Bulletin of Missionary Research.

[21] *President of the Companions Lighthouse for the Science of Islamic Law*, Libya http://www.youtube.com/watch?v=xdVnILalpeo, viewed on January 7, 2010.

[22] Garrison.

[23] Ibid.

[24] Ibid.

[25] Ibid.

[26] http://www.theforgottenways.org/apest/

[27] Dr. Alan Hirsch and his books, *The Forgotten Ways: Reactivating the Missional Church*, and *The Shaping of Things to Come: Innovation and Mission for the 21st Century Church* provided the genesis for the thoughts in this chapter. I appreciate his thinking and teaching on the APEST paradigm.

[28] *What Does a Healthy Church Look Like?* From *5 Stages for Multiplying Healthy Churches*, Greg Kappas and Henry Oursler, Grace Global Network Publications.

[29] I am indebted to Dr. Steve Holt, pastor of Mountain Springs Church in Colorado Springs, Colorado, USA, and the founder of Word and Spirit Churches International, for the content in this introduction.

[30] *How to Help Fulfill the Great Commission*, Transferable Concepts by Campus Crusade for Christ, p. 2.

[31] This chart was developed by Dr. Henry Oursler in his personal Bible study.

[32] Much of this material came from Tom Constable, *Notes on Acts*, http://www.soniclight.com/constable/notes/pdf/Acts.pdf, 2010 edition; Nelson's Bible Commentary, Radmacher, Allen, and House

[33] *Introducing World Missions*, A. Scott Moreau, Gary R. Corwin, Gary B. McGee.

[34] *First Clement 5:7*, written AD 95, perhaps the earliest known orthodox Christian writing after the New Testament was completed.

[35] Eusebius, *Ecclesiastical History*, 2.22

[36] Dr. Greg Kappas, President of Grace Global Network, International Church Planters Summit, Vizag, India, 2007.

[37] *How Does a Pastor Build an Evangelistic Church?* Jim Donohue, Sovereign Grace Ministries.

[38] Ibid.

[39] *The Jesus Film* is a movie that was produced by Campus Crusade for Christ, International. It is the most widely seen movie in the history of the world and is a very effective tool in reaching people with the Gospel who have never heard of Jesus. Missionaries take the movie into remote villages and show the film, and afterwards give an invitation for people to trust Christ as their Savior.

[40] Bob Roberts, *Glocalization*, Zondervan Publishers, p, 26.

[41] *The Radical Reformission*, Mark Driscoll.

[42] St. Francis of Assisi

[43] *Glocalization*, p. 30.
[44] Ibid.
[45] William R. Bright, *How to Help Fulfill the Great Commission*, Transferable Concept Series, Here's Life Publishers.
[46] E.M Bounds, Prayer
[47] Curtis Vaughn, *Expositor's Bible Commentary, Colossians*, Frank Gaebelin, General Editor, Zondervan Publishing House, p. 222.
[48] Observed during my internship with Josh McDowell, Campus Crusade for Christ.
[49] *Out of the Saltshaker and Into the World*, Rebecca Manley Pippert, InterVarsity Press.
[50] Curtis Vaughn, *Expositor's Bible Commentary, Colossians*, Frank Gaebelin, General Editor, Zondervan Publishing House, p. 222.
[51] Dr. Rice Broocks, writing a guest column in Ed Stetzer's blog, www.edstetzer.com, August 5, 2010.
[52] Ibid.
[53] Dallas Willard, *The Great Omission*.
[54] Ibid.
[55] Ibid.
[56] A.W. Tozer, *The Knowledge of the Holy*, p, 6.
[57] Alan Hirsch, *The Forgotten Ways*.
[58] LeRoy Elms, *The Lost Art of Disciple-Making*, NavPress.
[59] A.W. Pink, *The Holiness of God*.
[60] Bill Hull, *The Complete Book of Discipleship*, NavPress.
[61] Ibid.
[62] A.W. Pink, *The Holiness of God*.
[63] Ibid.
[64] The basis for most of this chapter is Robert E. Coleman's excellent book, *The Master Plan of Evangelism*, which is really a book about discipleship.
[65] Robert E. Coleman, *The Master Plan of Evangelism*.
[66] Ibid.
[67] Greg Herrick, *Go and Make Disciples of All Nations*, a transcript of a sermon on www.Bible.org.
[68] Robert E. Coleman, *The Master Plan of Evangelism*.
[69] Howard Hendricks, recorded speech at the "Making Disciples" conference, October 1983.
[70] See *The Disciple-Making Pastor*, Bill Hull, Baker Book House; The Complete Book of Discipleship, Bill Hull, NavPress.
[71] See *The Disciple-Making Church*, Bill Hull, Baker Book House; The Intentional Church, Randy Pope, Moody Publishers.
[72] All the pictures in this chapter are adapted from a Navigator's resource website: www.Resources@Navigators.org.

Made in the USA
Columbia, SC
29 January 2018